Some Aspects of the Life and Work of Nietzsche

LONDON
Cambridge University Press
FETTER LANE

NEW YORK · TORONTO
BOMBAY · CALCUTTA · MADRAS
Macmillan

TOKYO
Maruzen Company Ltd

Some Aspects of the Life and Work of Nietzsche, and particularly of his connection with Greek Literature and Thought

BY

A. H. J. KNIGHT

*Fellow of Trinity College and
Lecturer in German in the
University of Cambridge*

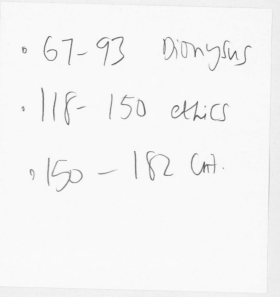

- 67-93 Dionysus
- 118-150 ethics
- 150-182 Crit.

CAMBRIDGE
AT THE UNIVERSITY PRESS
1933

CONTENTS

PREFATORY NOTE

I OWE a debt of gratitude to many who have helped me with advice and encouragement while writing this book. In the first place to the late Professor K. H. Breul and the late Professor J. G. Robertson; to Professor H. A. Korff, of the University of Leipzig; to Dr H. F. Stewart, Professor C. D. Broad, Professor F. M. Cornford, and Professor D. S. Robertson, all of Trinity College; to Mr E. K. Bennett, of Gonville and Caius College, Mr G. M. Sargeaunt, Mr H. W. Heckstall-Smith, the Syndics of the University Press, and several others. Last, but not least, to my wife.

A. H. J. K.

August 1933

CHAPTER I

Introduction

SINCE the outside world first began to take notice of the "hermit of Sils Maria", the critical literature about his work has grown steadily, until to-day it would be impossible for one man to survey it all, unless he should dedicate his whole life to the task. But such devotion would be unprofitable, for much of the Nietzsche literature is of poor quality. German critics have no doubt produced more books about Goethe or Shakespeare, but it seems likely that Nietzsche occupies the third place in their interest: yet much of the work devoted to him is markedly inferior to that written about other great thinkers and poets.

Yet Germany has also given the world a certain number of exceedingly interesting and stimulating works about Nietzsche. I shall have occasion to refer to most of these again before long, and for the moment I will do no more than mention with respect and admiration such critics as Bertram, Richter, Meyer, Riehl, Landsberg, and Oehler, not forgetting the philosopher's sister and biographer, Frau Förster. France, too, has contributed great things to the study of Nietzsche. Andler's immense work is the most valuable ever written on the subject, and other French critics (such as Lichtenberger) have, as is their wont, shed brilliant light upon it. Brandes in Denmark, Castiglioni in Italy, and others, have also done excellent work, so that the low average level of continental Nietzsche criticism is at least relieved by a fair number of illuminations.

But the English-speaking nations have contributed little of any value. England (and in a lesser degree America) is still backward in the study of modern humanities, and in no respect more backward than in German literature. But when we admit that, it still remains strange that these countries, which have turned out good work about Goethe, Schiller, Heine, and others, should have taken so little interest in this most interesting and important thinker and poet. It is largely a result of this that Nietzsche is commonly regarded in

England as a hypocrite, a fool, or a knave (even in circles where he is not confused with Treitschke, and accused of having plotted the war), whereas he was in actual fact a distinguished scholar, an extremely valuable (and generally accurate) critic of his times, a bold speculator, and, as a rule (though not always), a reasonably sensible man.

It is partly for these reasons, but chiefly as a result of a deep (though not uncritical) interest in the works of Nietzsche, that I have ventured to write this book, which, for the rest, makes no special claim to be original or exhaustive, but is meant to be accurate, impartial, and objective. I do not claim that it is more than a study of "some aspects of Nietzsche's life and works", and though I have from time to time put forward some new suggestions, there are few for which I would dare to claim great importance.

The method which I propose to adopt in order to discuss these aspects of the philosopher's work is to examine them in considerable detail, backing up my examination by frequent and long (translated) references to the author's text. Before I do that, I will give a short account of the life of Nietzsche, and a statement of the circumstances, chronology, and principal contents of his various books. This seems to me to be very necessary in view of the general ignorance of these outlines, especially for students of German literature. Then shall follow a more detailed investigation. This centres in part round Nietzsche's connections with Greek literature and philosophy; indeed this book originated some years ago in a dissertation which only set out to examine that side of Nietzsche's work: but I am not now confining myself to a discussion of these connections, although such a discussion would be profitable, and would afford material enough for more than one book.

The rest of the enquiry falls into three main sections. The first of these deals with Nietzsche's attitude and opinions concerning early Greece in general, and especially the pre-Socratic philosophers, contrasted with whom are Socrates and Plato.

The second main section deals with the three most important points in the speculative philosophy of Nietzsche himself. These points are to some extent developments of the opinions which I shall have considered in the preceding chapters. They are (*a*) the philosophy of Dionysus, as Nietzsche himself calls it; (*b*) the eternal recurrence, Nietzsche's theory of a cyclic universe; (*c*) the celebrated or notorious Superman, and the conceptions most nearly allied to him. I shall try to examine all these ideas with care and without prejudice, and confine myself principally to seeing what Nietzsche really said, at various stages in his career, not, at this point, to criticising it all. It will be necessary, in a great degree, to make use of the actual text of Nietzsche's books.

The third section will be critical. It will consist (*a*) of a somewhat sceptical examination of the value of Nietzsche's speculations, and of the probable effect of trying to put them into practice (it must always be remembered that he professes to intend them to be put into practice, and to think that it is, or should be, possible to do so); and (*b*) of an examination of a matter which seems to me of peculiar interest and of great importance, namely, the nature of Nietzsche's pessimism or optimism, and the problem whether he was altogether sincere or untroubled by misgivings about the value or truth of his speculations. Finally, I shall try briefly to summarise the main conclusions which I have reached.

This, then, will be exactly what it claims to be, a study of certain aspects of Nietzsche's work, but by no means of all. To write a complete and exhaustive study of him, using all the care and exactitude which are desirable, would be nothing less than a life's work. But the matters which I desire to look at are of some importance, and it may be that a gleam of fresh light can be shed on a few of them.

Here it seems advisable to make a few suggestions about Nietzsche's possible value, and his general characteristics. If the reader casts a glance over these at the outset, he will know more or less what to expect, and ought to be in a better position to pass judgment on the many remarkable phenomena which he will later meet. Such suggestions are meant to be in the nature of hints and warnings which shall open his eyes to possibilities or probabilities, and give him a few unmistakable direction-posts to begin with, before he is allowed or compelled to plunge off into trackless morasses of speculation and mysticism.

We have by no means settled whether Nietzsche belongs to literature or philosophy, or at any rate we have not decided the precise nature of his importance in either or both of these fields. It would seem advisable to make some effort at solving these questions before we go on to look into his life and opinions at short range.

It can be said at the outset that he is not a logician at all, and that his contribution to critical philosophy is negligible. He cannot argue: he has no method, no mathematical or quasi-mathematical system: no deep interest, even, in any domain of thought except ethics: and even in the field of ethical speculation he is a declaimer rather than a thinker. His whole system is built upon a void. He premises nothing to begin with, and it is often impossible to know what is to be assumed or taken for granted. Indeed, in different places one finds him assuming different and incompatible bases for his speculative construction, and one is frequently uncertain, even when he is in his heyday of intellectual and moral strength, what exactly he means his readers to understand by a number of his terms. Yet even so, admitting all this—and there is much more yet which could justly be brought against him as a philosopher and a logician—even so there remains a fairly solid substratum of worth that is not purely literary. His place in literature is assured beyond cavil: both as a poet and a prose-writer he is in the very first flight of his own country and indeed of all others, but that is certainly not his only value. The tendency to-day is rather to insist on this literary value,[1] even to exaggeration (for it is difficult justly to put him above Goethe), and to say that as a philosopher he merits little consideration. This is no doubt partly a reaction against the wild Nietzsche-philosophy-worship which went on for many years from about 1900, but partly, indeed mainly, I suppose, it is due to a genuine and largely justifiable

[1] This was of course written before the German "national revolution" of 1933. It is impossible to predict what will be the effect of the revolution upon Germany's future opinion of Nietzsche.

feeling among scholars, that there is far too much in Nietzsche which is mere words or mere imagery, poetry, extravagance. There is, I say, something in all this: but on the other hand I think it well to insist that there is actually much truth, sense, and sound speculation in Nietzsche, and that his social and ethical teaching has far more in it than has commonly been admitted by sensible people. These have usually seized upon the exaggerations and denounced them (reasonably enough, as a rule), just as less sensible people have uncomprehendingly applauded them: but they have missed or minimised the sense, the truth, the biting and invaluable criticism of contemporary (and often of universal) institutions. For it is as a critic of his times and of human folly that Nietzsche has great value: as a satirist he may be ranked with the greatest, as a destroyer he is unrivalled, as a constructive speculator he is usually inadequate or impossible, as a technical critical philosopher he is almost worthless. His temperament is not favourable, and he had an impossible burden of ill-health, disappointment, loneliness, and despair to contend with: small wonder then that he went mad at the age of forty-five: and small wonder that his temperament and his peculiar difficulties are continually cropping out in his work, and spoiling many of his best beginnings. For his faults are numerous and glaring, and such as to put off many a would-be impartial critic at the very start. He is treacherous and cruel: he has no sense of humour and no sense of proportion: he is undisciplined, one-sided, intellectually lazy, and spiteful: but he never writes better (and seldom more alluringly) than when he is exhibiting these imperfections in their most flagrant aspects.

It is next desirable to spend a short time in considering the influence which Nietzsche has exercised, in the forty years or so since Brandes introduced him to the notice of the world as a personality and a thinker to be taken seriously. There is no doubt that the literature and thought of modern Germany are dependent upon his influence more than upon any other single factor. It is probably true that Goethe is again beginning to assert his unshakable claim to dominate the spirit of his people, but it is equally true that for a number of years Goethe's influence was under a slight but definite cloud. It is, however, improbable that in the long run Nietzsche will usurp Goethe's position, and it would certainly be most improper that he should. Schiller is in a very different situation. He has now little hold on the intelligence or the affections of the German nation, though he remains (fatally, perhaps, for his reputation and his true merits) the idol of the old-fashioned schoolmaster. No doubt he is now unduly criticised, just as fifty years ago he was absurdly over-rated; and the pendulum will swing again in the other direction: but it seems quite impossible that Schiller can ever again become the German national poet. For the decline of his popularity Nietzsche is to some extent responsible, though, as Andler has shown, Schiller exercised a powerful influence upon him.[1]

But as Schiller's influence faded, from 1900 onwards, Nietzsche's grew beyond all bounds and all reason, and nearly every poet of any pretensions fell under his sway. One cannot understand or criticise Hofmannsthal or Stefan George without appreciating their dependence on Nietzsche, nor can one imagine that the modern tendencies in German literature, some of them admittedly of little value, could have developed without the new creative and critical impulse which he gave. The Nietzsche Archive at Weimar, the mass of Nietzsche research which has been conducted, the societies which have been formed around him as around Goethe, are only further tokens of the importance which he has attained, and I need not dwell upon them. His influence has been most powerful and most continuous upon highly educated young men, such as university students. The earliest and strangest proof of this was afforded by the impromptu speech of thanks and veneration delivered at his funeral by a student in the name of all German youth.[2]

[1] Nietzsche, *Sa vie et sa pensée*, vol. I, chap. II.
[2] His influence upon German scholarship (especially literary criticism) has been no less remarkable. Fritz Strich begins his epoch-making work upon German Classicism and Romanticism with the

Outside Germany Nietzsche's influence has been greater than that of any other modern German writer, and perhaps proportionately greater than in Germany itself. He has been translated into most European languages, and has been studied all over the world. He was first brought into prominence, at a time when Germany would not hear of him, by the lectures of the Danish critic Dr Georg Brandes; and Mr Bernard Shaw was one of the first who commended him to the world.

One of the objects of this book is to discuss Nietzsche's connection with Greek literature and Greek thought. It is probable that his dependence on Greek philosophy was even more continuous and intimate than the best critics have allowed: but I do not claim that this dependence can be rigorously proved. It is extremely difficult to tie Nietzsche down to anything: he is a creature of wild and wayward moods, inconsistent, forgetful, and often untruthful: and however clear are the signs which point in one particular direction, when one is trying to trace his spiritual ancestors, the trail is often confused or obliterated, and it is well-nigh impossible to attain certainty in the quest.

One of the more recent and most interesting authorities, Ernst Bertram,[1] begins with a chapter, entitled "Ahnentafel", in which he discusses Nietzsche's peculiar historical sense. The special point which he raises has a curious and appropriate connection with Nietzsche's Hellenism, to which it forms a suggestive introduction. There is no doubt that Nietzsche felt himself peculiarly connected with the past; not only with the past of classical antiquity, but with various

following sentence: "Since Friedrich Nietzsche uttered his mighty protest against the science of history, which, through its devotion to a dead past, cripples the plastic, myth-creating power of the German man, the science of literary history, too, meets, in Germany, the most various doubts about the value and importance of its problems; and what historian will not have been tormented before now, in hours of contemplation, by such thoughts?" An extremely good summary of Nietzsche's influence (following upon a most valuable, lucid, and fair account of his work) is given by one of the outstanding German thinkers of recent years, Ernst Tröltsch, in *Der Historismus und seine Probleme*, chap. III, section 6 B (pp. 506–7 in the Collected Works of 1922).   [1] *Nietzsche*, Berlin, 1922.

men or epochs or causes. Though he is in one sense a revolutionary, he is in another an admirer and upholder of tradition, the tradition of those whom he revered as great men, whose heir he felt himself to be, and whose work (or his own interpretation of it) he wished to carry on. His spiritual ancestors are not always the same, but, whoever they are at any moment, he always feels drawn to them by a tie of special, intimate kinship, and not merely by intellectual influence.

If one turns to those examples of this historical sense which have a particular relevance to Nietzsche's Hellenic affinities, one will be well on the way to establishing that he positively felt himself to be the heir and supporter of *a* Greek tradition (not of *the* Greek tradition), a pious descendant, not a critic. "My pride is: I have a long descent, therefore I do not need fame. I have long lived in the thoughts which moved Zarathustra, Moses, Muhammed, Jesus, Plato, Brutus, Spinoza, Mirabeau, and in many things that which needed some thousands of years as an embryo comes for the first time mature to the daylight in me." That is, "I am the heir of all the past, right back to the beginnings of wisdom". And so: "If I speak of Plato, Pascal, Spinoza, and Goethe, I know that their blood runs in mine—I am proud, when I speak the truth about them—the family is good enough not to need to invent or to conceal: *and so I stand to everything that has been....*" In *Jenseits von Gut und Böse* one finds a kind of Platonic or Heraclitean conception of philosophers: "Under an invisible spell they continually run *the same circular course again and again....* Their thought is in fact far less discovering than recognising again, remembering again, a return, a return home to a distant primeval household of the soul. To this extent philosophising is a sort of Atavism of the highest rank". In *Menschliches, Allzumenschliches* the same thought occurs in regard to artists: "A magnificent remnant, to whom, as to some wonderful stranger, on whose strength and beauty the fortune of former times hung, we pay honours such as we cannot easily grant to our equals. The best in us is perhaps inherited from feelings of former ages, which now we can hardly reach directly".

It appears from these singular passages that Nietzsche considered Greek literature, Greek life, and Greek thought from the unusual and unphilological standpoint of a Greek born out of time, not from the standpoint of a normal critic. Further evidence in favour of this contention will appear from time to time when I am considering individual problems and single books, and here I only wish to add this: that, when Nietzsche admires Wagner as the supremely great artist, he praises him (so everywhere in *Die Geburt der Tragödie*) because he is the Greek tragic dramatist reborn: that, when he abandons Wagner, and becomes a Positivist, he styles himself, for a while, the descendant of Socrates: that, in his creative period, he christens his creation in the name of Zoroaster *and of Dionysus*. Each stage is presided over, so to speak, by some figure of the Greek world; and always Nietzsche's own attitude is the attitude of a disciple. "I am a disciple of the philosopher Dionysus", he said in his last book.

On the more general subject of his instinctive demand for continuity, there is still something to be added. It is often little but pure superstition, but it cannot all be dismissed as such. Bertram, who, so far as I know, discovered it, seems to exaggerate it, and to write a good deal that is rather extravagant around it to support his thesis of the duality of Nietzsche's nature. But apart from this, one can find many instances, mainly in *Ecce homo*, of the inordinate importance which Nietzsche attached to certain coincidences: to the fact that his father was born in Eilenburg on the day on which Napoleon entered the town; that he himself had the same abnormally slow pulse as Napoleon; that he entered his name on the books of the University of Leipzig one hundred years to the day after Goethe,[1] and so on. One can find many such passages, but I only propose to mention some which are connected with Wagner. Wagner is especially important in a study of Nietzsche's Hellenism, because, up to 1878,

[1] "I cannot say what a refreshing effect this chance occurrence had on me; undoubtedly it was a good omen for my Leipzig years, and the future has taken care, that it should have a right to be called a good omen."

Nietzsche associated—or confused—him with Dionysus. Of the close of his association with Wagner, on the appearance of *Menschliches, Allzumenschliches*, Nietzsche writes, in *Ecce homo*: "When the book eventually came into my hands in its finished form...I sent amongst others two copies to Bayreuth. Through a miracle of design in chance there simultaneously reached me a beautiful copy of the text of *Parzival*, with Wagner's dedication to me...'to his dear friend Friedrich Nietzsche, from Richard Wagner, Kirchenrat'. This crossing of the two books—it seemed to me as if I heard an ominous sound with it. Did it not sound as if *swords* were crossing? So, at any rate, we both felt: for we both kept silence". Of *Zarathustra* he writes: "The closing part was finished exactly in the sacred hour in which Richard Wagner died in Venice"—and he speaks in a similar tone, in a letter to Peter Gast, about Wagner's death: "The news of his death has just come from Genoa. I started out to-day without any reason, and just bought, contrary to my custom, the evening edition of the *Caffaro*, which had just appeared. My first glance falls on the telegram from Venice".

I have spent some time in echoing Bertram's discussion of Nietzsche's peculiar historical sense, because it seems to me desirable that it should be borne in mind, while examining his ideas and his books more closely. It is possible—I would dare to say it is probable—that many of his oddities (which eventually become insanities) are traceable to this no doubt mistaken belief that he is the exclusive heir of all the ages, and particularly of the ages of Greek culture: but if his faults and manias are traceable to this belief, so are many of his virtues, such as that queer, exalted, inspired accuracy with which he sees distant epochs and alien characters, and with which, also, he criticises the barbarisms, prejudices, and inanities of the nineteenth century. When all is said and done, the fount of his genius remains inexplicable: but it is undeniable that he possessed genius, and Bertram's approach to understanding it through his peculiar sense of history and of kinship with the remote past is the most hopeful that I have yet encountered.

CHAPTER II

An outline of Nietzsche's life, activities, works, ideas

Nietzsche was born at Röcken, near Leipzig, on October 15, 1845; and as this day was also the birthday of his father's benefactor, Friedrich Wilhelm IV of Prussia, he received the king's names. The veneration with which he later regarded his namesake, and his satisfaction in the coincidence of their birthdays, are small, but characteristic instances of his determination, which we have already noted, to feel himself part of a Tradition.

We will not embark upon a lengthy or exhaustive sketch of his life,[1] but we shall do well to pass fairly rapidly over the main points, and to select a few of these for extra attention before we proceed to our more detailed investigations. In particular we must look at one or two facts which bear upon his Hellenism. His career as a classical scholar is not the most important side of his life, and his philological works are neither of the very highest value in themselves, nor are they the most essential material for this study: but much of his Weltanschauung is only intelligible in the light of his close and long preoccupation with classical literature, so that it is essential to see something of the form which his philological activities took. It also seems desirable to give, in this section, an outline of his philosophical works, their development and shape, and to speak shortly of the circumstances in which they were written.

Nietzsche's father and grandfather were both Lutheran ministers—who *may* have been of Polish descent—and his mother's family, too, were clerical. A consequence of this, we find, is that even in the midst of his most vehement attacks

---

[1] There are several good biographies. The best are perhaps those by Andler, Richter, and Frau Förster. For bibliography see appendix.

on churches and priests, he never forgets to feel a certain close
kinship with them. To this kinship he ascribed a special knowledge of priests and priestcraft, which, in reality, he did not
possess. Nor does he ever quite lose a sense of respect towards any clergy or saints except the early Christian Fathers.
So he says in a letter of 1881 to Peter Gast: "From my child-
hood days I have pursued it (Christianity) into many corners,
and I believe I have never in my heart been grossly dis-
respectful towards it". He says the same more strongly and
more picturesquely in *Zarathustra*: "Here are priests: and
even if they are my enemies, I pray you go quietly by them
and with sleeping sword...my blood is akin to theirs: and
I desire to know that my blood is honoured in theirs too".
Similar passages are found in several other places.

In 1849, Nietzsche's father, whom he always regarded with
peculiar reverence and affection,[1] and whose life he believed
to be curiously linked with his own, died after an accident.
The mother went to Naumburg, her birthplace, with her two
young children, whom she brought up carefully and piously
with the aid of various female relations. All of these facts
combined to make the boy's personality and development
quite unusual.

The next milestone in his career was his admission as a
scholar at the famous boarding school of Schulpforta. Here
he acquired the unusual proficiency and interest in the classics
which led straight to his professorship and to his own philosophy. In his later life he does not say very much about
Schulpforta, and what he does say is not especially flattering.
In *Ecce homo* he speaks of it, together with several other
places in which he lived during his early years, as "a place
of misfortune for my physiology". There is no record in this
autobiography, where one would expect it, of any great
benefits conferred upon him by his education at the school:
but in not owning to any, Nietzsche, neither for the first nor
the last time, shows himself unjust and petty. We know in fact
that he was happy at the school, and that he worked pro-
digiously hard and most successfully. A fairly full record of

---

[1] See the most curious portrait of his father in *Ecce homo*.

his classical studies at the school has been kept, and in the limited Musarion edition of his works (which includes every known fragment), all that survives of the essays and other writings which he turned out while at school or university has been collected in the first volume.[1] This volume, there-fore, is a psychological document of the first order concerning Nietzsche the philosopher.

Nietzsche was at Schulpforta from October 1858 until September 1864. In these years he studied classics with much success and mathematics with no success at all. The later Nietzsche had a soul above logic if anyone ever had, and he never succeeded in proving any contention scientifically. One could hardly have expected that he would ever have been a mathematician or scientist of any merit. It is clear that from early youth he disliked rational argument. This characteristic accounts for most of his value—and for most of his weak-nesses. Interesting, too, and symptomatic of his later develop-ment and interests, is the *Germania*, a literary and philo-sophical society numbering three persons (Nietzsche and two friends). Among the publications of the *Germania* are various essays or passages which foreshadow some of his more famous later problems. The classical authors whom he admired most at this time were Plato and Aeschylus; the German authors Wagner and Hölderlin. Nietzsche's relations to Hölderlin[2] have been investigated by more than one student, and, im-portant though they are, we will not go into them now. Much the most valuable product of these early years is Nietzsche's work, done when he was a Primaner of twenty, on Theognis. This essay is of the highest importance to any student of Nietzsche's own philosophy, because it seems to mark the first occasion on which his attention was called to the possible relativity of the conceptions of good and evil. Thus it is

[1] The second volume of this admirable edition, which in all comprises some twenty-two, contains Nietzsche's earlier lectures and other works after his appointment as professor at Basel in 1869.

[2] Hölderlin is the most genuinely Greek poet in all German literature, and he resembles Nietzsche (or Nietzsche resembles him) in many ways.

really the first step towards his final, central thesis of Super-morality (Herrenmoral) and Slave Morality (Sklavenmoral), on which so much of his thought depends.

Nietzsche left Schulpforta, and went to study at Bonn, with the intention of being a philologist. While at school he had apparently played with the idea of being a musician, but under-went a reaction against it, which caused him to take up philology. He says: "In a word, I desired a counterpoise to my former changeable and unquiet tendencies, I desired a science which could be pursued with cool reflectiveness, with logical coldness, with equable work, without at once cutting at one's heart with its results". This statement is of unusual significance and interest in view of Nietzsche's later desertion from Wagner to the scientists, also a change from emotion to reflection, from music to criticism, from enthusiasm to cold-ness.

The most powerful university influence on Nietzsche's work, and perhaps on his personality, was the famous classical scholar Ritschl. After Nietzsche had spent two terms at Bonn, Ritschl quarrelled with one of his colleagues and moved to Leipzig. Nietzsche, though he believed him to be technically in the wrong, was unwilling to lose the benefits of his supervision, and followed him thither. In Leipzig Nietzsche began at once to make himself a great reputation as a classical scholar. His most important works were another essay on Theognis, *Zur Geschichte der Theognideischen Spruch-sammlung*; and one *De Fontibus Diogenis Laertii*, a successful composition for a university prize, also published in the *Rheinisches Museum*. This work does not contribute so richly as the Theognis essay to our understanding of Nietzsche's Weltanschauung; but it is worth noting that his interest in Diogenes Laertius—not a specially inspiring writer—was due to his subject—the lives and opinions of the ancient philo-sophers. Thus in all reasonable probability this essay affords yet another instance of Nietzsche's increasing devotion to the study of Greek philosophy, rather than any other side of ancient literature.

This is confirmed by certain other pieces of work which

he is known to have undertaken at this time; by his interest in Democritus; by his unsuccessful Doctor-Dissertation on *Die Grundschemen der Vorstellung*, and that which he planned, but never wrote, on *Der Begriff des Organischen seit Kant*; as by the idea, conceived at this time, of writing a history of literary studies in the ancient world.[1] To this period belong also the beginnings of two of his early and important enthusiasms—Wagner and Schopenhauer. Schopenhauer he discovered by accident (as he himself maintained, by one of the significant coincidences of his life) and he adopted his Weltanschauung with great enthusiasm, though he was not in full agreement with every detail. He especially approved of Schopenhauer's ideas on the Will and on Überwindung— overcoming—while a practical effect of his philosophy was that unusual regard for friendship which is characteristic of Nietzsche now and all through his life. Wagner he met personally during his time at Leipzig. From that moment he was a supporter of his views, and a lover of his music. Their really close association did not come until Nietzsche was at Basel, but it was anticipated and desired, at any rate by Nietzsche, before he went there.

Nietzsche's university career was interrupted by military service,[2] which lasted for one year, and was mainly occupied with the dangerous consequences of an accident. In the autumn of 1868 Nietzsche returned to Leipzig, and resumed work there as a private teacher, in the hope that he would receive an appointment on the staff of the University, after obtaining the doctor's degree for which he was working.

Instead of the appointment at Leipzig, for which he was preparing himself, there came the totally unexpected call to Basel. Leipzig granted him his degree without further examination, and he left Germany, hardly ever to return. At Basel he began as Extraordinarius, but was promoted after he

[1] For the evidence see his letters of these years.

[2] This was just after the Austrian war of 1866. There were already signs of coming trouble with France, and the Prussian Government, in real or affected nervousness, was cancelling exemptions from service. But for this, Nietzsche (who was already short-sighted) would not have served, and might never have lost his health.

had been in office a short time. The appointment had been influenced by the excellence of his published philological articles,
reinforced by a glowing recommendation from Ritschl.

Basel was the second great break in Nietzsche's life. Schulpforta gave him his initial chance of a good career, by affording
him totally unusual opportunities. Hence he became a
scholar. Basel did something just as important, by removing
him from the Reich and the nationalistic influence of its
Universities. Some years later Nietzsche wished to return to
Leipzig, not so much out of love for Leipzig as out of his
desire to play again an active part in the affairs of education
and research. But by that time he had abandoned almost every
German idea or thought or characteristic, so that, even had he
returned, he could never again have become his former self. But
indeed this very desertion of his traditions and his nationality,
more than any other factor, caused the attempt to fail.

Thus far Nietzsche has been a schoolboy or a student. Now,
at the astonishingly low age, for a full university professor,
of twenty-four, he becomes a teacher. At heart he remains a
teacher for the rest of his twenty years of active life. In the
first decade he is partly a philologist and partly a philosopher:
in the second he is purely a philosopher. There then remain
another eleven years during which he is hopelessly and para-
lytically insane.

Nietzsche's lectures[1] during his professorship are interesting and fairly widely known. They are also of considerable
importance as a contribution to the understanding of his
other work. His Inaugural Lecture, delivered on May 28,
1869, was entitled *Homer und die klassische Philologie*. This
work is important psychologically rather than philologically,
for, while it contains nothing epoch-making about the
questions of Homer's personality and the authorship of the
Homeric poems, there is in it much which helps us to understand Nietzsche's later work and general standpoint. He is

[1] The lectures themselves, or notes and fragments concerning
them, have been collected and edited in full in the Musarion
Monumental-Ausgabe (vols. II, IV, V, VI, VII), and some of them
are also available in other editions.

curiously on the defensive: peculiarly concerned, for one in his position, to defend philology against its critics, above all to protect it from the charge of laying irreverent and destructive hands on the delicate bloom of poetic beauty. He describes the peculiar charm of Hellenism as "Indescribable simplicity and noble dignity", a definition which is in violent contrast with his later conceptions, but approaches very closely to Winckelmann's or Schiller's. He goes on to state, clearly and convincingly, the main facts and arguments in the Homeric problem, and to give his own solution; ending, as he had begun, with a defence and praise of philology.[1] The last sentences are the most memorable and the most significant. In words which define his whole attitude to philological science at this period, he concludes:

> *Gratitude* we demand,...in the name of philology herself, who indeed is neither a Muse nor a grace, but a messenger of the gods; and as the Muses descended to the sad, tormented Boeotian peasants, so she comes into a world full of gloomy colours and pictures, full of deepest and most incurable pains, and tells consolingly of the fair bright shapes of the gods of a far, blue, happy land of magic....A philologist too it well becomes to compress the goal of his endeavour and the way to it into the short formula of a confession of belief; and so be this done, in that I turn a sentence of Seneca around as follows: "Philosophia facta est quae philologia fuit". Therewith is meant, that each and every philological activity should be enclosed and hedged about with a philosophical view of life....

Philosophy is already uppermost in his mind. The "philosophical view of life" is the essential. Without it philology is of little value.

Nietzsche's work at Basel was interrupted by the Franco-Prussian war. Naturalised Swiss as he now was, Nietzsche insisted on taking the only part in it that was open to him, that of a hospital orderly. While serving in this capacity he conceived, so he tells us, the idea of *Die Geburt der Tragödie*: or rather worked out, "under the walls of Metz", the problem of the "alleged serenity of the Greeks and of Greek art", with which he had previously wrestled in some corner

[1] "Life is worth living, says Art, the fair seductress; life is worth understanding, says Science." This is the opening sentence of the lecture—a striking and typically Nietzschean beginning.

of the Alps. But the campaign brought results which were even more important than this book, for during it Nietzsche fell dangerously ill with dysentery. For ten years afterwards he was in continual bad health, and all the rest of his life he was never robust. How much of the subsequent development and character of his thought can be ascribed to sickness has not really been determined; and I do not propose to follow up the question here. It seems certain that from his own weakness, and his fight against it, arises very much of his adoration of perfect—Greek—health, power, vitality. It is also certain that he realised that his own long and partly successful struggle against illness was a true example of "Wille zur Macht", to which conception his experiences must have contributed much.

He returned to Basel an invalid, but went on with his work, with intervals in which he had to retire and recuperate; and shortly after his return came the publication of *Die Geburt der Tragödie*, which marks the beginning of a fresh period, that of creative authorship. Before saying anything about this, I propose to discuss shortly his remaining philological work and the other products of his professorial career, though chronologically most of these come later. Although he was in continual ill-health, attacked, on some two hundred days in each year, by terrific and incapacitating headaches, he continued to undertake about thirteen hours of work a week. There is a fairly long list of the lectures which he delivered, and much material remaining from them: but I do not propose to go into them very minutely, as their importance is not of the first order. However, if we appreciate the extent and range of Nietzsche's interests in the field of classical thought, and note the many problems which he touched as a philologist, it is much easier for us to understand how he came to fill his own work with cognate ideas, and to see why he *must* have done so. The actual lectures, as collected in the Musarion edition, are as follows: *Sophocles' Oedipus Rex; History of Greek Rhetoric; The Diadochoi; History of Greek Literature; Rhetoric; Greek religious observance; The Greek lyric poets; Aeschylus; Hesiod; The pre-Socratics; Plato; Quintilian;*

Cicero; and the important treatise (which of course is not philological) *Über die Zukunft unserer Bildungsanstalten*. There are also certain published works not in the form of lectures, some of which are of considerable importance. These are: *Beiträge zur Quellenkunde und Kritik des Diogenes Laertius*; a critical edition of the so-called "Contest between Homer and Hesiod", in two forms; three essays about Rhythmics; notes on Democritus; an Introduction to the study of Classical Philology; an Introduction to the study of the Platonic Dialogues; *Wir Philologen*, an important fragment; and *Die Philosophie im tragischen Zeitalter der Griechen*, which is still more important, though likewise fragmentary.

This is practically the full list of Nietzsche's philological work, up to the illness which forced him to resign his post in 1879. I venture to suggest that for breadth and real soundness of interest this will stand comparison with the majority of programmes worked through by classical lecturers anywhere. And though these works are not epoch-making like some of the philosophical books, they are nearly all unusually challenging and valuable. The angle from which Nietzsche regards classical antiquity is novel; and it remains fairly constant throughout his life. So, though I shall have occasion to comment in more detail on certain points coming under this category, when I discuss some of the main later works and ideas, I do not think that it would be out of place to say here a few words about his general outlook, and about some of the single books.

We find at once that when Nietzsche is giving his own opinions freely—there is naturally a marked difference in spontaneity between his professorial and student utterances— he shows a marked scepticism about the ultimate value of philology, and indeed of all scientific study. We have seen how concerned he is, in the Inaugural Lecture, to justify his existence as a philologist, and we have noted that he only does this by defining the aims of philology in a very unorthodox way. The tendency culminates, so far as the critical works are concerned, in *Wir Philologen*, which was written in order to lay down definitely the proper aims and scope of classical study. It is very largely a refutation of false conceptions of antiquity, for instance of the idea that the Greeks were a civilised and humane people in a modern sense. The remarks which we find here about the inhumanity of the Greeks are incidentally of considerable importance for any theory (such as we shall discuss in due course) that the later Superman is of Greek origin; because Nietzsche describes a race which most remarkably resembles that strange conception, and supports his description, against the more general views of scholars, by unusually careful argument. What, he says, is the good of philological study which lacks poetical inspiration? What is the good of anything which has not an essentially poetical motive? Ought philological study or any study to aim at anything except "the education of the great individual"? This is exactly the problem which occupies the later books, and the answer is exactly the same. His reason for supporting classical education, theoretically and in practice, is given in the sentence: "For the education of great spirits antiquity is more powerful than ever before". Thus, if a man pursues research for its own ends, if he lacks the touch of poetry with which he can inspire other people, if he fails to bring out the greatness of classical literature and *ancient life*, he has no right to be a philologist. Science by itself has no place in the world. It must only exist as the servant of art or the servant of life. This is exactly the view which we find in *Die Geburt der Tragödie* and the *Unzeitgemässe Betrachtungen*; and it precisely coincides with the ideas of the Zarathustra period. Only in his curious, contradictory, but very sane middle years, 1876 to 1882, does Nietzsche seriously diverge from this standpoint. It is intelligible enough that the forcible expression of these and similar views should not have contributed to make him popular among philologists; and it is a fact that after the appearance of *Die Geburt der Tragödie* he was never again taken into account as a serious classical student, to the great discredit of his critics.[1]

[1] Only Erwin Rohde, one of the greatest of all classical scholars, remained his friend and admirer. Rohde's epoch-making book *Psyche* owes much to Nietzsche's ideas.

Another point which is conspicuous in these early works is Nietzsche's attitude towards the Greek philosophers. This too is unusual; and, like his ideas on the comparative value of science and art, is reversed in the middle period of his work, only to be taken up with increased vigour in the last.[1] For Plato—or rather Platonism—particularly as inspired by Socrates, "the destroyer of the Greek world", he has an intense and rather spiteful dislike. Platonism is "the worst, most wearisome, and most dangerous of all errors". Plato himself is his own absolute antithesis, the perfect anti-Hellene. The mission of Socrates and Plato, he says, was to secure the control of all the instincts by the reason: his own creed, at this time, was the unchecked dominance of natural instincts. Life is "Will to Power"; and it is only men like Socrates, who are mean and base ("Socrates was Mob"), who deny that it is rightly so. Socrates is the end, the deliberate destroyer, of all before him that was fine and admirable, of the glorious myths, of tragedy, music, lyricism. He is the first and completest decadent: "The danger of the Greeks lay in virtuosity of all kinds; with Socrates the virtuosi begin". Nothing in him is comprehensible to Nietzsche except his irony, and nothing admirable except his death.

But Nietzsche's attitude towards Socrates' predecessors is quite different. Much of his own thought has its foundations in the pre-Socratics, and he continually and consistently admires their personalities and their systems. Empedocles, for instance, was to be the hero of a drama which he projected, but never wrote;[2] and Heraclitus, above all others, he always mentions with particular admiration and respect. "The world eternally needs the Truth, so it eternally needs Heraclitus." Heraclitus in fact is the only thinker who could possibly have taught some of the essential conceptions of his own later Weltanschauung, such as Recurrence and Dionysus.[3]

[1] For a detailed discussion of these very important matters, see below, chap. III.   [2] Cf. Hölderlin, once more.

[3] It is perhaps hardly necessary to warn the reader, in anticipation of the fuller discussion in Chapter III, that Nietzsche, in praising the pre-Socratics, often praises them for things which he *read into* their sayings, not for what those sayings (probably) contained.

But in general Greek philosophy in these early days is enjoying its real period of greatness; and the period comes to an end with Socrates, who ruins the whole sequence of thought and tradition.

This enthusiasm for the period of Greek philosophy which is generally dismissed as a period of mere preparation (or of mere superstition) is characteristic of Nietzsche. He has the same sympathy for other manifestations of the period of growth, and comparatively little for the classical age of Athens. Tragedy, for example, that is to say what is commonly meant by Greek Tragedy, the work of the dramatists of the Periclean age, is to his mature mind a slightly decadent product of an extremely decadent age. Aeschylus he still admires: but after Aeschylus there sets in at once the age of Reason, culminating in Socrates, who finally kills Tragedy. Homer, too, exerts no great attraction upon Nietzsche. Homer is the incarnation of the Apolline spirit, as defined and explained in *Die Geburt der Tragödie*, and the Apolline spirit is by no means the ideal. Nietzsche's Greece (we cannot insist upon this too strongly) was the period after Homer, after Hesiod, and before Aeschylus, the age of *lyric* poetry, and of the *Tyrants*. The lyric poet and the tyrant together make up a great part of the Übermensch-Zarathustra-Dionysus ideal. From his admiration for Archilochus, for Theognis, and for Peisistratus, Nietzsche derived a more definite and more passionate enthusiasm for the lyric and for the view of life which the lyric represents (or which he thought that it represents). From this enthusiasm he goes on to the conception of Dionysus, and thence to the Superman.

In these days, when he still admires Wagner and Schopenhauer, Nietzsche often speaks of the revival of his favourite period of Greece in them. They are united in their common inspiration by a tragic Weltanschauung to which, in spite of his supposed revolt against pessimism, Nietzsche always remained faithful. It is because of this tragic Weltanschauung (which has nothing in common with the corruption of Tragedy by Sophocles, Euripides, Socrates, and Aristotle) that he admired pre-Athenian Greece. Hence in writing about pre-Socratic philosophy, he speaks of it as "die Philosophie im *tragischen* Zeitalter der Griechen". The whole history of Greece was a tragedy, for its splendid beginnings deteriorated, were atticised and made sterile, so that the promise of the early days was never fulfilled. This idea was novel enough when Nietzsche first expressed it, and of course it met with universal contempt or hostility, but twentieth-century scholars[1] seem by no means disinclined to take a similar view.

Nietzsche understood the Greeks better than their humanitarian admirers had done. In this early period *Wir Philologen* expresses most forcibly his belief that Greek culture was not humane or philanthropic, and that it was in many respects not what the present day would admit to be culture at all. Only in the late *Götzendämmerung* does he express anything but dislike of Greek politics. The development of the Greeks, he says, was interrupted in the middle, by the victory over the Persians in 480, which made Athens supreme, and thus prevented the older culture from developing or even existing any longer. "Greece was bound to be ruined after the Persian wars...." Athens was the least naturally artistic and philosophical of all the Greek states. But all critics had fallen into the conventional error of admiring the moderation and proportion aimed at and attained in Athens, crystallised in the injunction μηδὲν ἄγαν at Delphi; and it was held that these qualities, these laws, were typical of all Greece, not merely of Athens in the later fifth century. But Nietzsche's ideals are immoderate and extreme,[2] and he saw these qualities and values prevailing in most of Greece. "Moderation is foreign to us", he says in *Jenseits von Gut und Böse*. He is not consistent in this belief, but it seems to be inherent in his final convictions. Where a work of art originally came into existence through the coincidence of the principles of moderation (the Apolline principles) and of immoderation (the Diony-

---

[1] Miss Jane Harrison was one of the earliest to do so in England.
[2] Not always. In his middle period he is enthusiastic about "moderation". Cf. *Morgenröte*, aphs. 109, 215.

siac), the end is the complete victory of the latter. We find this best in *Die Geburt der Tragödie*.

"Titanlike" and "barbarian" seemed to the Apolline Greek the effect which the Dionysiac aroused, though at the same time he could not conceal from himself, that he was inwardly akin to those fallen Titans and heroes. Yes, he was bound to feel more still; his whole existence with all its beauty and moderation rested upon a hidden basis of suffering and of knowledge, which basis was revealed to him again through that Dionysiasm. And see! Apollo could not live without Dionysus . . . the Muses of the arts of appearance paled before an art which in its intoxication spoke the truth, the wisdom of Silenus cried aloud "Woe, woe!" to the serene Olympians. The individual, with all his limitations and means, went under here in the self-forgetfulness of the Dionysiac states, and forgot the Apolline precepts. Excess revealed itself as truth, contradiction, the ecstasy born of pains spoke from the heart of nature about itself.

The foundations of Nietzsche's belief about Greek Tragedy are clear enough from these sentences. To one who felt thus the so-called golden age of Greece could not possibly be as interesting as the earlier times, which undoubtedly show less sense of proportion, more violence of desire and action, more and readier response to natural impulses, no self-questioning, no preoccupation with any sort of theory. Those were ages dominated by tyrants, who in some respects are very like the Nietzschean Superman. The tyrannic ideal seemed to Nietzsche to have been almost universal in those days, when the men who did not want to become political tyrants, that is, the philosophers, desired an absolute intellectual supremacy. Hence arose the disturbances and wars—a sign of real "Wille zur Macht". But the other side of Greek culture, the proportion and moderation and calm, clear beauty, usually acclaimed by Hellenists, Nietzsche neither appreciated nor admired; and we even find him occasionally suggesting that the Greeks, in their best moments, were really oriental. Dionysus-worship no doubt originated in the East; Zarathustra is of oriental origin; and it is probable that Nietzsche had elements in him which responded with especial sympathy to Asiatic stimuli: but the suggestion that Greek culture is "the first binding-together and synthesis of everything Eastern" is surely frantic nonsense. Elsewhere Nietzsche expresses the same thought by saying that the Greeks were really "barbarians of genius", and only to be admired as such.

With the reaction against Wagner came a change, though not a lasting one. In *Menschliches, Allzumenschliches* Nietzsche appears as an apostate against nearly all his earlier ideas, and makes Comte, Voltaire, Logic, Positivism, Free Thought his ideals. As one might therefore expect, he seems in this sceptical middle period to sympathise with the more traditional opinions about Greece, so that he even speaks kindly of Socrates. The period only lasted six years, and though it was sincere, it was not genuine. It was a reaction, not a conversion; but while it lasts, we find, not indeed for the first time, an outspoken admiration for the Sophists, whom, rather than Socrates and Plato, Nietzsche regards as the spiritual heirs of the old philosophers. "Our way of thought to-day", he says, "is in a high degree Protagorean." Gorgias is the first "Nihilist" of Europe, the first questioner of values, where he himself is the latest and most complete. The sub-title of *Menschliches, Allzumenschliches*, "A book for free spirits", and the whole "Freigeist" ideal, which is common to all three books of this period, seem to show a strong Sophist influence: and, no doubt, with this influence goes that of other sects, Cynics, Sceptics, and Stoics, who possess the power—a Nietzschean power—"voluntarily to give themselves a harder skin, to say in the storm: 'What matters this?'"

We have noticed that in his student days at Leipzig Nietzsche had discovered the philosophy of Schopenhauer, and had become for a time his enthusiastic follower. Later, that is by about 1869, he had taken up a more critical attitude, which consisted, roughly speaking, in assenting to Schopenhauer's main propositions, but rejecting certain details. Then Nietzsche fell more profoundly under the influence of Richard Wagner, who occupied much the same position in regard to Schopenhauer. The Weltanschauung which is such an important part of Wagner's chief operas is almost pure Schopenhauer. Wagner, it is true, is not such an extreme pessimist; but, like Schopenhauer (or to be exact, following Schopenhauer) he conceives the world as "Will and Idea", preaches the necessity of escaping from the bonds of the Will, and advocates quietism, though the mission of redeeming a bad world by good art, which by 1869 Wagner had undertaken, was an addition of his own, by no means in keeping with Schopenhauer's principles.

Nietzsche had met Wagner at Leipzig, and had been much attracted by the operas, and in particular by the *joie de vivre* of *Die Meistersinger*. While at Basel, as he had anticipated, he visited the composer and his wife, who were then living at Tribschen on the Lake of Lucerne, and got to know them intimately. The friendship was largely, though not entirely, founded on their common artistic ideals, and on the welcome admiration of Nietzsche for Wagner's work. How deep the latter was, is shown by the following extract from a letter of Nietzsche to Gersdorff, written in August 1869.

In addition I have found a man, who reveals to me, as does no other, the image of that which Schopenhauer calls "Genius", and who is entirely penetrated by that wonderfully intimate philosophy. ...In his neighbourhood I feel as if I were in the presence of the Divine.

What Nietzsche's admiration meant to Wagner we perceive from the following letter *à propos* of the former's lectures on Socrates and Greek Tragedy.

I have now no one, with whom I can take things so seriously, as with you, Her alone excepted....Do you remain a philologist, in order, as such, to let yourself be directed by music....Now do you then show for what end philology exists, and help me to bring about the great "Renaissance".

It was with the purpose of helping on Wagner's new renaissance, and of harnessing philology in his service, that Nietzsche, in an essay which he meant as the first section of a planned History of Greek Art, combined a striking idea about Greece and an ingenious theory about Wagner, to produce *Die Geburt der Tragödie*.

As Wagner propaganda of a refined and intellectual sort this work was a success, though not such a success as Nietzsche and Wagner believed: but as a work of philology it only brought Nietzsche into disrepute. Its chief critic was

Wilamowitz; but no classical scholar, except Erwin Rohde, had a good word to say for it, and the number of classical students at Basel suffered accordingly. Nowadays, though few people would follow Nietzsche in everything he says, many scholars would admit that he shows a great deal of fresh insight into Greek life, a great deal of rather fortunate accuracy, and a deep sincerity and love of Hellenism; while it is an almost universal opinion that the book, as a work of art, and as a piece of original thinking, is a real *tour de force*. One very serious criticism can be brought against it. There is no real connection between Wagner and Greek Tragedy, and the divagation into Wagnerian music at the end spoils the artistic unity and does not convince an unprejudiced reader. We shall return to *Die Geburt der Tragödie* in a later chapter.

Wagner was overjoyed with it. "*Die Geburt der Tragödie*", said Nietzsche later, "perhaps aroused the greatest note of joy in all Richard Wagner's life; he was beside himself, and there are things of marvellous beauty in *Götterdämmerung*, which he produced in this state of an unexpected and very great hope." Wagner said the same: "Since reading it I have been again working at my last act.... I do not for my part understand how I deserved to experience anything like this". The foundation of the Bayreuth theatre followed in the next year; and Nietzsche began his next work in the same spirit. In 1873 there appeared the first of four *Unzeitgemässe Betrachtungen*, essays, preluded by the lectures *Über die Zukunft unserer Bildungsanstalten*, which urge a regeneration of *German* culture in the sense in which Wagner worked for it. Originally Nietzsche planned twenty-four of these essays, but, after frequently changing the proposed number, he finally decided to write twelve, of which *Wir Philologen* was to have been one. The abandonment of the design when only four were completed was due to his reaction against Wagner and his breach with him.

None of these essays is very long. All are provocative, and some passages are violent. Number one, *David Strauss, der Bekenner und der Schriftsteller*, was the most controversial book that had appeared in Germany for years, and excited

floods of criticism and comment. It is an exceedingly powerful, though not deliberately personal attack upon the well-
known (at that time very famous) biographer of Christ. It
was called forth by Nietzsche's belief that, in the type of
German culture which Strauss represented, Germany was
threatened by the worst possible form of danger to any real
civilisation. The danger was mainly a result of the foundation
of the new Reich. Germany's sudden political splendour, her
triumphant campaign, her new national pride, led her into
a kind of impermeable self-satisfaction, an intolerable pseudo-
civilisation, a half-and-halfness and indifference to all things
of real cultural value, "a chaotic medley of all styles" for
which Nietzsche invented the magnificent term "Bildungsphilisterei"—"philistinism of culture". Strauss, author of
one of the most widely read books of the moment, is the ideal
"Bildungsphilister", and therefore he gets the full weight of
Nietzsche's attack. "Do not be superficial, whatever you
are", the book might be paraphrased, "but if you cannot be
anything else, do not commit the deadly sin of imagining that
you are civilised, or that you have any right to count at all.
Life is infinitely more complicated than you will ever know;
and Art, not Education, is the only thing which can teach
people to appreciate it."

The second essay, *Vom Nützen und Nachteil der Historie
für das Leben* (1874), sets out to trace the causes of "Bildungsphilisterei". Nietzsche claims that nothing except a mon-
strous mediocrity can be produced by mere knowledge, or by
any degree of intellectual and scientific learning unassisted.
He then finds that history, as taught in Germany, is ruined
more utterly than any other subject by a stupid insistence on
making it "scientific": whereas, studied in the proper way,
as a record of great men and great deeds, it can be a uniquely
valuable means of civilising people. As it is practised, there is
nothing more useless or more destructive: and nothing bears
more responsibility for the regrettable state of German
mentality. The competent and strong may study history with
profit: the mediocre and weak will lose something of the
little they have by doing so. "History can only be borne by

strong personalities; weak personalities it completely extinguishes. The historical sense, when it reigns uncontrolled, and draws its full logical consequences, tears up the roots of the future." The reception of the essay was cold, and even Wagner did not greet it enthusiastically.

Schopenhauer als Erzieher, of the same year, is, in contrast, a panegyric. It is really concerned with the question what form the culture of the future must take. What kind of person can contribute to producing it? The answer is—the exact opposite of a David Strauss, that is, a genius. Genius, Nietzsche goes on to say, is necessarily and essentially poetical: the production of genius is the one end and aim of civilisation. Love and enthusiasm for genius is the rôle of the average man; and it is in order to understand this that one should be educated on Schopenhauer, in whom one must recognise a heroic personality and a great mission well carried out. Of Schopenhauer's philosophical system we hear practically nothing: but again we come upon the ideal of a rebirth of pre-Socratic Greece, here associated with Schopenhauer.

Richard Wagner in Bayreuth is in many ways a repetition of *Die Geburt der Tragödie*. It is a hymn of praise to Wagner, on the same curious ground that Wagner's art is the rebirth of Greek art. "For me the phenomenon of Wagner, which I have seen in the flesh, explains, at first negatively, that hitherto we have not understood the Greek world, and conversely it is there that we find the only analogies to our Wagner phenomenon." It is noteworthy that even at the time when Nietzsche was writing this, he was planning the first anti-Wagner work; and the suddenness of the change which follows is at first sight a little disturbing. The explanation which he himself gave in *Ecce homo* (an explanation a little difficult to accept with the equanimity with which his greatest admirers take it) is that every time he speaks of Wagner, here or in any early work, he is really thinking of himself; that he is subconsciously giving an analysis of his own psychology, development, ideals, and achievement.

The breach follows quickly enough. It is no part of the present work to discuss its psychological difficulties and their interpretation. A statement of the main facts must suffice. Before we go on to them, we should do well to note that probably the driving-force behind the whole Wagner episode was Nietzsche's love of Greece, that his appreciation of Wagner the artist rests on two things: on personal friendship and on the presumed rebirth in Wagner of the great Greek tragic era. It was not really Wagner whom Nietzsche worshipped, but that which he took Wagner to be.

The first fundamental criticisms of Wagner's outlook occurred about 1874. The difference in Weltanschauung consisted, in a word, in Wagner's increasing tendency to Christian mysticism, at a time when Nietzsche was coming to a more independent standpoint as a result of his experience as author of *Die Geburt der Tragödie* and *Unzeitgemässe Betrachtungen*. Insuperable divergences soon revealed themselves on the following four questions: (1) Are Truth and Life inseparable? (2) Is Truth always in the interest of Life, and if not, which is to be preferred? (3) Do any absolute ethical standards exist?[1] (4) Is Life, as we know it, a thing to be accepted or rejected, applauded or condemned? *Richard Wagner in Bayreuth* was written rather against Nietzsche's will—that is perhaps why it is such an unmixed encomium— and when, after avoiding his friend for some time, the philosopher allowed himself to be fetched to the opening performances at Bayreuth, the reaction was completed. Nietzsche saw that the operas were not what he had taken them for, that the supporters of Wagner were not, in his opinion, cultured people, but "intolerable Germans" (in his later works they are often singled out for peculiar vituperation), and that Wagner himself was not his great ideal artist. *Parzival*—"Rome's belief without words"—completed the severance. Nietzsche and Wagner met and corresponded no more. Only in his last few works did Nietzsche really set out to attack his former friend, and then only on account of his increasing and, in his eyes, menacing influence. For his personal feelings towards him remained warm, and he always

[1] Wagner was in process of adopting the Christian doctrine on this point.

insists that Wagner's latent ability as artist and musician far exceeded that of anyone who had ever composed or written. The fatal mistake was that he had attached his work to a false philosophy, that he had been led away—by Christianity and by Germany. To one surveying the episode to-day the strangest thing is not that the relationship should have ended as it did, but that it ever should have existed as it did. This I can only explain by supposing, on evidence which seems to me sufficient, that Nietzsche's enthusiasm was not for Wagner, but for lyric poetry, and that the close friendship with Wagner was responsible for the connection of two totally incompatible things. One of the most significant passages which go to prove this is the fragment, already quoted to illustrate another point: "I desire to reckon Schopenhauer, Wagner, and the earlier Greek culture together. That gives a view of a magnificent civilisation". The "earlier Greek culture" and the "magnificent civilisation" were really important in Nietzsche's eyes: not Wagner or Schopenhauer.

Let us see what Nietzsche himself says about the actual breakdown. His own words are probably, for once, accurate as well as sincere. The passage is from the Preface to the second volume of *Menschliches, Allzumenschliches*, dated 1886, and reprinted as one of the sections of *Nietzsche contra Wagner*, with the heading

"How I got away from Wagner." As early as the summer of 1876, in the midst of the time of the first festival performances, I silently took leave of Wagner. I cannot stand anything ambiguous; since Wagner had been in Germany, he had been condescending step by step to everything which I despise—even to anti-Semitism.... It was indeed then high time and more to take leave: I very soon got proof of that. Richard Wagner, apparently the conquering hero, actually a despairing decadent who had become rotten, suddenly sank down, helpless and broken, before the Christian Cross....Lonely again now, and cruelly mistrustful of myself, I then took sides *against* myself—not without anger—and *for* everything which hurt precisely me, and came hardly to me: so I found the way back to that brave pessimism,[1] which is the opposite of all idealistic humbug, and also as it seems to me, the way to *myself*—to *my* task....

[1] This sentence is specially notable. Compare chap. VII.

"My task" follows in 1878, in the form of *Menschliches, Allzumenschliches*, which, with *Morgenröte* and *Die fröhliche Wissenschaft*, composes the middle period of Nietzsche's work, reversing the first, and itself reversed by the third, like the world periods in the Politicus Myth. Nietzsche has now become a Positivist and a Cynic: he upholds Socrates instead of the pre-Socratics; he begins to question nearly every accepted proposition and convention in the world, and he sets out on a furious search for Truth at all costs. As the period progresses, we find fewer question-marks, a reversion to anti-Socratism, a more creative tendency; and finally the prophetic figure of Zarathustra, at the end of *Die fröhliche Wissenschaft*. Moreover, Nietzsche no longer writes in the form of essays, but in brilliant, cutting, deadly aphorisms, inspired, as he said in *Götzendämmerung*, by Sallust.

Menschliches, Allzumenschliches was mainly written during a year's leave of absence from university work, at a time when Nietzsche's health was very bad indeed. It was finished in some haste on the centenary of the death of Voltaire, to whom it was dedicated. By a curious coincidence it appeared at exactly the same moment as *Parzival*. The dedicatory verses expressed Nietzsche's hope, undoubtedly sincere, that Wagner would not take offence at his change of view, but it was immediately evident that the breach was final. Most properly, neither Nietzsche nor Wagner said anything about it at all. Shortly after the book had appeared, Nietzsche gave up his professorship.

The distinguishing characteristics of this "book for free spirits" (which was much the most independent work that Nietzsche had yet produced) are (1) the social ideal of "the good European" (really another term for "the free spirit"); (2) the higher valuation set upon Scientific Research than upon Art—most curious and most significant; (3) the thesis that the Will is not free, that all things happen in accordance with immutable universal rules, and that therefore men cannot be judged as if they were responsible for any of their actions; (4) the further stage in the same argument, that there is no such thing as "Sin" or "Guilt" in the religious sense;

(5) the relentless pursuit of Truth; (6) the consequent momentary but decided admiration for Socrates; (7) the introduction of the principle of "ordering men in ranks". There are countless other points, for *Menschliches*, *Allzumenschliches*, which includes the originally separate *Wanderer und sein Schatten*, is Nietzsche's longest book: but these are the most important.

Here, for the first time, we find Nietzsche strongly anti-Christian. It is noticeable that he attacks Christianity as the supplanter of Greece. It is also worth noticing that in this book he emasculates or vitiates his criticisms from the very start by attacking it on the ground that it *is already* a dead religion (not that *it deserves to be*) and therefore a mere useless encumbrance.[1]

Although there is not the same direct relationship between the theme of this work and Greece, as in *Die Geburt der Tragödie*, yet one finds in every other section or so some reference or other to Greek life or literature, or an expression of some opinion about them. The whole work is intensely cynical, in which it is unlike any other of Nietzsche's writings; but it is not unnatural that a book which came into existence in the circumstances of *Menschliches*, *Allzumenschliches* should have such a tone. The cynicism, one should add, is of a genial and pleasant kind. It is particularly noticeable that in the book itself, as it stands, Wagner is practically never mentioned. The condemnation of all that he represents is purely implicit: but in the unpublished fragments and sketches the attacks are strong and open. Moreover, these attacks, even at this early stage, when they lack the slightly artificial—or at any rate calculated—fury of *Der Fall Wagner*, are largely based on Wagner's *lack* (now) of the qualities of the ancients. We find: "Wagner's uncertainty in his final aims, *unantique* mistiness".[2] We find a comparison—which shows how completely Nietzsche lacked a sense of proportion—of the character of Philoctetes with those of Wagner's operas, from which he concludes that there is not much character-drawing in

[1] E.g. in aph. 26.
[2] Frag. 428, Musarion Monumental-Ausgabe.

Wagner; and so on. In the fragments, which are very important, though they lack the artistic fineness of the published parts, there is an approach to the teaching of the *Phaedrus* and the *Symposium*, in the insistence laid upon friendship, which is conceived in a form like the Platonic Eros.[1] Again, when Nietzsche praises Voltaire, he praises him for possessing the Greek quality of "Proportion";[2] and, speaking of the scientific qualities, which he now rates higher than any other, he says that Europe owes them all to the Greeks.[3] Even when he is discussing virtues, he selects for special praise precisely those which an aristocratic Greek of the earlier period would have considered καλὸς κἀγαθός: "Good-humour, friendliness, courtesy".[4]

Menschliches, Allzumenschliches is rather a dangerous book. The chief danger lies in the great profusion of thoughts, which follow on one another so closely that one often cannot see the wood for the trees, that one is led astray by brilliant and irrelevant details. It also illustrates another general failing of Nietzsche's, his inability to maintain a high level throughout a book, for the later parts of Book I—the original work—fall far below the first sections. Nor is Nietzsche yet a really original thinker. He is groping and tentative, and hence unnecessarily destructive. He was certainly aware of this later, on the evidence of the Introduction which he wrote in 1886; and it is with a further passage from this Introduction, concerning the purpose with which this very important book was written, that we will for the moment take leave of it.

Thou shouldst become lord over thyself, lord also over thine own virtues. Previously *they* were thy lords; but they must only be thy tools alongside other tools. Thou shouldst gain power over thy For and Against, and learn and understand how to hang them in and out....Above all thou shouldst see with thine eyes, where injustice is always greatest: namely there, where life is at its smallest, narrowest, most needy, most elementary stage of development, and yet cannot avoid taking *itself* as the end and measure of things, and for the sake of its own preservation secretly and pettily and

[1] Cf. frag. 477.   [2] II, 221.
[3] II, 265.   [4] I, 49.

ceaselessly crumbling away what is higher, richer, greater, and questioning it—thou shouldst see the problem of ordering in ranks with thine eyes.

"With this book begins my campaign against Ethics" (*Ecce homo*). This book is *Morgenröte*,[1] which appeared in 1881. After Nietzsche had resigned his professorship, his life consisted in his philosophical work and nothing much else. He changed his place of residence every few months, to suit his health, living mainly in Sils Maria, in Turin, in Nice, but only visiting Germany for very short intervals. In *Ecce homo* he has given an interesting and thorough account of his climatic needs and the effect of residence in various places; and from the following passage in a letter one gains a fair idea of what his different habitations meant to him:

Do you know Turin?...Here everything is arranged in a free and broad manner, including the squares, so that in the midst of the town one has a proud feeling of freedom. Hither have I dragged my load of cares and philosophy....The neighbourhood of the mountains guarantees a certain energy, even roughness. Then comes the turn of my old summer-residence Sils Maria: the Upper Engadine, *my* landscape, so far from life, so metaphysical. And then a month of Venice....

But the outer circumstances of life are not of great importance to him: the great thing is his work. "What still now remains to me of life (little, I think) must give entire and full expression to that for the sake of which I have held out at all."[2] Nietzsche's health reached a crisis in 1879, but then improved spasmodically. In 1882 it was very much better, and we find as a consequence the unwontedly joyous tone of *Die fröhliche Wissenschaft*. Later on it relapsed at times, but never deteriorated to the level of 1879, until Nietzsche suddenly went mad in January 1889. These last years were very lonely, and it is largely to this loneliness, added to the effects of years of ill-health, and of his failure to awaken any interest in his speculations, that his mental breakdown must

[1] Sub-title: "Gedanken über die moralischen Vorurteile".
[2] From a letter.

be attributed.[1] His old friends were largely lost to him: and he made no new ones to take the place of Wagner. His former colleagues turned hostile to the revolutionary thinker; and his sister, having married a man whom he disliked and despised,[2] went to South America. The only recognition which came to Nietzsche in all these years was from Georg Brandes, in Copenhagen. The rest of the world waited until he had gone mad, before it began to notice him without contempt.

Morgenröte is an improvement on *Menschliches, Allzumenschliches* in several respects. It is less tentative, less cynical, more constructive, and better arranged. We find a new emphasis laid on "distinction of behaviour" as a very high virtue. From this emphasis will develop later the philosophy of Superman, Supermorality and "Will to Power". The general trend is the same as that of the last book, and the differences, though I believe they are important, are only differences of application. As in *Menschliches, Allzumenschliches*, Nietzsche insistently demands the abolition of the conceptions of guilt and punishment. He also lays much emphasis—which was not to be found in former works—upon "Proportion and self-control" in all things,[3] and we find a curious tendency to laud Epicureanism at the expense of other philosophies of life. A strange little point is an aphorism (no. 36) devoted to the praise of modern times as against earlier ones. Interesting, too, is aphorism 114, where Nietzsche indirectly explains the change in his methods and ideas by the psychology of the sufferer whose sufferings give him a far clearer and deeper insight into life than is possessed by a healthy man. When a man is well, he has illusions. When he is sick, he loses them, because he sees things as they really are. When he regains his health, he begins to have them again. Nietzsche himself is now beginning to regain his health, and with it the illusions or ideals.

[1] Also to the established fact that he took chloral, as a means of overcoming sleeplessness. Perhaps he was syphilitic, but that has not been proved.

[2] The anti-Semitist leader Förster. Nietzsche always detested anti-Semitism.

[3] Cf. aph. 215.

If we are interested in tracing his connections with the Greeks, we should do well to note the contrast[1] which he draws between the Greek and the German "Virtues". It is significant, because he claims as the virtue of virtues among the Greeks precisely that quality which is evident in the books of this middle period.

Personal distinction—that is the ancient virtue. Submitting, following, publicly or in secret—that is the German virtue.... Greeks and Romans felt otherwise... it was part of their southern freedom of feeling, to guard against "unconditional confidence" and to retain in the last recess of their heart a slight scepticism against all and everything, be it god or man or idea. That is just the ancient philosopher. "Nil admirari"—in this sense he sees philosophy. And a German, namely Schopenhauer, goes so far in the opposite direction, as to say "admirari id est philosophari".

The four cardinal virtues, too, are: "To be honest towards ourselves and to whatever is our friend; brave against our foes; generous-minded towards the conquered; courteous—always".

One of the most instructive passages in the whole book is the last paragraph, which affords us more insight into Nietzsche's objects than any other single extract.

All these bold birds, which fly out into the distance, the farthest distance—somewhere, certainly, they will be able to go no farther, and will cower down upon a mast or a barren cliff—and be so grateful too for this pitiable shelter! But who would have the right to conclude from this, that there exists *no* huge free path any more in front of them, that they have flown as far as one *can* fly!... *Other birds will fly farther!* This our insight and faith flies with them, competing with them beyond and above... and sees the flocks of birds far stronger than we are, ahead, which will strive to go whither we are striving, where everything is still sea, sea, sea!... And whither then do we want to go? Do we indeed want to go beyond the sea? Whither are we torn by this mighty longing, which is worth more to us than any pleasure? Why just in that direction where hitherto all the suns of humanity *set*? Will they say in our memory one day, that we too, *steering to the West, hoped to reach an India*—but that it was our lot to be wrecked on Eternity? Or, my brothers? Or?

There follows, in 1882, *Die fröhliche Wissenschaft*, a book similar to *Morgenröte*, but more joyous, in consequence of the

[1] Aph. 207.

improvement in Nietzsche's health. Let us again glance at the most relevant passage in *Ecce homo*.

The "Red of Morning" is a book which says "yes", deep, but bright and kindly. The same is true again and in the highest degree of the "Gay Science": in almost every sentence of it depth of feeling and caprice are to be found tenderly holding hands. A verse, which expresses my gratitude for the most wonderful month of January which I have ever experienced, betrays sufficiently from what depths "Science" has here emerged in order to become *joyous*. . . .

Nietzsche is here as determined as ever to attack the foundations of all existing ethical systems, as insistent as ever on the relative nature and the unaltruistic origin of all "Virtues": but there are many signs of a return to something like the idealism of his first works. This tendency becomes particularly evident in the last section of all, which introduces the figure of Zarathustra, and in the accompanying poems— *Lieder des Prinzen Vogelfrei*. *Die fröhliche Wissenschaft*, says Nietzsche in the Preface of 1886,

that means the Saturnalia of a spirit, which has patiently withstood a fearful long pressure—patient, stern, cold, without submitting, but without hope—and which now is suddenly overwhelmed by hope, by the hope of health, by the intoxication of recovery. . . . This whole book is simply nothing but a fit of cheerfulness after long abnegation and impotence, the rejoicing of strength returning, of belief newly awakened in a to-morrow and a day after to-morrow, of the sudden feeling and inkling of a future, of near adventures, of seas open again, of goals again permitted, again believed. . . .

The philosophy of the book we might sum up in two sentences, the one, γνῶθι σεαυτόν; the other, "do not sympathise with your neighbour, but rejoice with him".

With this the second period ends. Before we pass on to *Zarathustra* we should do well to look back upon it very briefly. Its principal value consists in Nietzsche's much more scientific treatment of his problems. In this way, indeed, the Positivistic period is the ideal preparation for the more genuinely creative last years. This Nietzsche expressed very well in a sentence from the fragments to *Menschliches, Allzu-menschliches*. "It is necessary to take up the whole of

Positivism into myself and yet still to be the representative of Idealism." He did this—it was a great and unusual achievement and in doing so he achieves a certain nobility of scepticism, if one may so call it. Life is an experiment—"an experiment of the man who strives to learn the truth". It has not cheated him, he says: year after year he finds it richer and more desirable, because he has recognised its essentially experimental character, and that it is not "a duty, a fate, or a deceit." The man who sees that this is the essential nature of life can live "not only bravely, but even joyously, and laugh joyously too".

Nietzsche has scientifically attacked the prevalent standards of ethical values, which, he has said, are based upon caprice, self-interest, and the desire of the weak majority to maintain themselves at the expense of the desirable few. Religion, especially the Christian religion, is condemned on the same ground, that its moral tenets are calculated to promote the mentally and physically bad. Truth and life are not natural friends, and do not co-operate in any way. Truth is generally incompatible with the enjoyment of life, which it sometimes entirely destroys, yet the pursuit of Truth is man's highest aim.

The influence of Greek thought, and Nietzsche's interest in it, are nearly as marked in the second period as in the first, but they take new forms. We do not find so much discussion of problems of Greek life as in *Die Geburt der Tragödie*: but much light is thrown upon matters concerning Greece, in odd remarks. The opinions are often in striking contrast to those of the first period. This is most glaring in regard to Socrates, who, at any rate in *Menschliches, Allzumenschliches*, is in high favour. The reason is clear enough. The change from *Die Geburt der Tragödie* to the middle period is in effect a change from Heraclitus to Socrates; and when Nietzsche praises scientific study as the highest of man's intellectual activities, he is logically bound to take the side of its protagonist in Greece.

Also sprach Zarathustra begins the third period; but it is really a work apart. It is a poem rather than a work of philosophy, in spite of the philosophy which it contains. It was written in three parts, the first in the early days of 1883, the second a year later, and the third almost immediately after that. Each of these was completed in about ten days. Part four was written between the end of 1884 and February 1885, but not publicly printed until 1892. None of these made any stir at all. What little interest they excited was wholly unfavourable; and from now on Nietzsche had to get his works published at his own expense.

Zarathustra is an extraordinary work in every respect; not least in the manner in which it came into the world. The first three parts were written in a kind of ecstasy, which Nietzsche describes in a very memorable passage of *Ecce homo*.

Has anyone, at the end of the nineteenth century, a clear conception of that which poets of strong ages called *Inspiration*? ·If not, I will describe it. If one had in one the slightest relic of superstition, one would hardly be able to defend oneself against the feeling that one was merely an incarnation, a mouthpiece, a medium of overpowering forces. The conception of Revelation, in the sense that suddenly, with indescribable certainty and refinement, Something becomes visible, audible, Something which overwhelms one and overturns one in the depths of one's being—this alone describes in simple words the state of affairs. One hears, one does not seek; one takes, one does not ask who is giving; like a flash of lightning a thought occurs to one, with necessity, in its form without hesitation—I never had a choice. An ecstasy, the colossal strain of which periodically relieved itself in a flood of tears, which makes one's steps now rush madly, now move slowly, a state of being entirely outside oneself....This is my experience of inspiration; I do not doubt that one must go back thousands of years, in order to find anyone who can say to me: "It is also mine".

The form of *Zarathustra* is unlike anything that comes before or after it. Instead of the aphorism, we have a highly poetical rhythmic prose, resembling that of the Psalms, and, like them, divided into verses. The chapters are nearly all short, and their number is large. The language and style are most remarkable. Nietzsche never had written anything so exquisite, nor did he do so again. Chiefly for these reasons, *Zarathustra* has become much the most widely read and most famous of his books, and those persons who have a little, but only a little, first-hand knowledge of his work, have nearly always gained it from *Zarathustra*. This, in a way, is right and proper: it is his most beautiful work, and it is his philosophy *in nuce*: but it is also his philosophy in its most deep, difficult, and dangerous form, so that it requires more careful study than any of his other books. It is everywhere easy to commit serious mistakes of interpretation; and there are some essential passages which it is impossible to understand fully without several very close readings. Nietzsche realised this, indeed he probably intended it to be so: but later, seeing the misunderstandings which were current about *Zarathustra*, he planned a systematic and unambiguous account of his speculations in *Der Wille zur Macht*. It is a very great loss that the design was never carried through,[1] for in its present form *Der Wille zur Macht* is an imperfect and unsatisfactory book, which does not make clear all that Nietzsche intended.

Also sprach Zarathustra contains two main conceptions, both entirely new, and a large number of others which arise directly from them. Of the main conceptions the first is the Superman. There have been indications in earlier books that Nietzsche's thoughts were tending in the direction of this theory: but really, in spite of these, the idea is suddenly flung at the reader as a new revelation in the beginning of *Zarathustra*: "God is dead! Now let us will that the Superman live!...Man is a thing that must be excelled". In his second period Nietzsche had paid much attention to Darwin and ideas of evolution generally. Partly from these, and partly by a reversion to the conception of Dionysus, for whom Zarathustra is practically another name, he conceives the ideal of a biological and intellectual development of man to another being, in comparison with whom we shall be what the ape is in comparison with us. "What is the ape in the eyes of a man? A source of laughter or of painful shame. And that is just what man must be for the Superman: a source of

---

[1] When Nietzsche went mad, he left *Der Wille zur Macht* in the form of masses of incomplete, unco-ordinated, and contradictory MS. notes, which have since been arranged and edited in different ways by different people.

laughter or of painful shame." To this higher state of existence man, as he is at present, can and must progress, for "that which is great in man, is, that he is a bridge and not an end: that which can be loved in man, is, that he is a transition and a setting". We ourselves are the only creatures who have power to produce the Superman, for we are the only things on earth with consciousness and will. The things which stand in the way of such a progression must be abolished. Such are quietism, passive virtue, pessimism, morality as preached by professional moralists, literature, which teaches acceptance of representation instead of fact, the state, and its pillars, society. All these are forces which tend to prevent the advance. When these first obstacles are out of the way the future will lie open to the creative man, and from him the Superman will in time proceed. Each individual man must advance through self-mastery, progression beyond himself, a progression directed by his own will, beyond rules laid down for him by others. Here again we find something which the Greeks would have understood and applauded—we must progress beyond pity. Pity cripples action. It achieves nothing and even prevents achievement.

Ah, where in the world were greater follies done, than in the neighbourhood of the compassionate? And what in the world caused more suffering than the follies of the compassionate?

God is dead; God died of his pity for man—

Therefore be warned against pity: from it comes a heavy cloud yet upon men!...

But mark this word too: all great love is yet above all its pity, for it desires yet to create that which is loved....[1]

But all creators are hard.

Does not this sound like an echo of many things, essential things, in Greek literature, of the words in the *Oedipus Tyrannus*, of the *just* Kreon to the blinded Oedipus, or of the claims of the artistic city of Athens in the Melian Dialogue? That this hardness was really inherent in Greek social

---

[1] All this is clearly reminiscent of Plato's *Republic*, both in ends and means. Platonic, too, is the exaltation of Friendship in this book, Friendship, which makes impossible, not love, but sensuality.

standards, is far more widely believed now than in Nietzsche's time, but he himself was intensely conscious of it.

After this Nietzsche proceeds to declare war on priests, as preachers of asceticism, on "virtuous" people, whose ideal is mediocrity, on the lower classes, "the mob", and on all who are content to live without an ideal, preachers of equality, philosophers who uphold the existing order of the world. Through self-mastery first we can learn how the ideal may be reached, but next through something more important and more unusual, through realising *that all things recur*.

This is the second important new idea in *Zarathustra*. It is really quite new, though suggestions leading up to it have already been found in other places. Why has Nietzsche conceived such an apparently far-fetched idea? Not primarily on scientific or logical grounds, but for his own peculiar ethical reasons. To the strong man, the knowledge that everything must exactly repeat itself for ever will be the strongest imaginable reason for courage, gaiety (not optimism), and will to greatness. This Nietzsche has previously explained, hypothetically but clearly, in *Die fröhliche Wissenschaft*. We shall probably be disposed to raise at once the objection that it becomes useless to attempt to progress, since the cosmos is inevitably doomed to revert to the older and lower form as the wheel turns. The Superman will only lead back to the ape, and so on *ad infinitum*. Nietzsche has foreseen and tried to refute this in the last sections of *Die fröhliche Wissenschaft*:

Would you not throw yourself down, and gnash your teeth, and curse the spirit, who spoke thus? Or have you ever experienced a tremendous moment, in which you would answer him: "You are a god, and never heard I anything more divine!" If that thought were to get power over you, it would change you, as you are, and perhaps crush you; the question, at each and every thing: "Do you desire this yet again and yet countless times?" would be the greatest weight that could lie on your actions! Or how satisfied would you have to become with yourself and your life, in order to desire nothing more than this last eternal confirmation and sanction?

Zarathustra triumphantly asserts the splendour of this idea. Recurrence is the greatest "Yes" to life as we find it, based on the most passionate enthusiasm for the world, to the extent of desiring and applauding its unceasing return in exactly the same cycles.

From this point Nietzsche progresses without hindrance to the culmination of the book in the long chapter "Von alten und neuen Tafeln", where the new ideals and new thought are summed up in their relations to all aspects of life. This is in the third book. The fourth book has little to add, but serves as a recapitulation.

The figure of Zarathustra, of whose sermons, speeches, and actions the book consists, is nominally that of the Persian sage more familiarly known as Zoroaster; but there is really little connection between them. The name is a name and no more: though there is evidence in *Ecce homo* to show how Nietzsche regarded Zoroaster and Zoroastrianism.

I have not been asked, what precisely in my mouth, the mouth of the first Immoralist, the name Zarathustra means: for that which composes the tremendous uniqueness of that Persian, is exactly the opposite of Immoralism. Zarathustra first saw the real wheel in the mechanism of things in the struggle of the Good and the Evil—the translation of morality into the metaphysical as Power, Cause, Purpose in and for itself is *his* work. Zarathustra *created* this fatal error, morality: therefore he must also be the first who *recognises* its true nature. Not only that he has here longer experience and more experience than any other thinker...the more important point is that Zarathustra is more truthful than any other thinker. His teaching, and his alone, sets up truthfulness as the highest virtue....The overcoming of morality by itself through truthfulness, the overcoming of the moralist by himself and his transformation into his opposite—into *me*—that is the meaning in my mouth of the name Zarathustra.

The book is justly famous both as a work of art and as a work of speculative philosophy. But it is well to emphasise once more that its speculations are often very easy to misunderstand, and therefore very dangerous. Yet it is a wonderful achievement, and the more it is read, the deeper it appears. The ideas which it contains are mainly unaltered in the works which follow, though these, reverting to the earlier aphoristic style, set out to argue critically what Zarathustra proclaimed poetically. The last of all, *Der Wille zur Macht*, was designed to supplement *Also sprach Zarathustra*, and this fact alone shows how slight is the alteration or development in the principles of Nietzsche's last period. We find that the remaining books emphasise different sides of Nietzsche's thought (which is never finally systematised), and this at times in a striking degree: but there is nothing out of harmony with its general trend.

Consequently, we may legitimately survey these last works more rapidly than we have treated the others, for though they are all interesting, and contain much important matter, not one of them is epoch-making. *Jenseits von Gut und Böse* explains itself by its title. Written in 1886, it endeavours to survey the chief fields of human activity, and to show how in all of them morality is an expression of that will to power which is the sole driving-force in the cosmos. There is no such thing as an absolute ethical standard. Everything which is hailed as good or as evil is only good or evil according to the standpoint of those who invented the morality, or of those—generally the weak numerical majority—who made it current as a means of protecting themselves and of satisfying their own will to power. This double morality is the theme of *Zur Genealogie der Moral* (1887), in which Nietzsche argues with great brilliance that everything can be traced back to the old fundamental division of mankind into slaves and masters, aristocrats and mob. Hence we have two original ethical systems: "Herrenmoral", based upon the aristocratic values—beauty, strength, courage, power, and all that increases these, even if it is not what the world generally calls good: and "Sklavenmoral", based on the values of the mob, which is weak and contemptible, but strong enough, thanks to its numbers, to assert itself and get its scale of values recognised and accepted as a universal morality. Such a "Sklavenmoral" is the very essence of Christianity—the values of the mob are exactly the Christian values—and therefore Christianity must be one of the first things to be abolished. Not that the slave values, *for the slaves*, are bad. In fact, for them, they are the best possible. Therefore it will always be the rôle of the numerical majority to be governed by this scale, and to live in submission to the strong. For the strong *can* rule, and therefore *must*: they *can* rise above the limits of an ethical code, and therefore *must*. But here modern civilisation is hopelessly at sea, because in it the majority have got everything into their hands, and have succeeded in imposing their ideas on all the world.

After *Zur Genealogie der Moral* comes *Der Fall Wagner*, a bitter attack on the composer. In itself it was not nearly so important, but it brought serious consequences for Nietzsche, for it lost him some of his few remaining supporters, who could not endure the tone in which he attacked a former friend. It is also noteworthy as the book in which certain authorities—those who do not contend that Nietzsche was always insane—have detected the first symptoms of exaltation, peculiarity, perhaps madness. Not long afterwards followed *Nietzsche contra Wagner*, a collection of criticisms culled from various places in the philosopher's other works. This did not appear publicly until 1895. In the summer of 1888 (actually before *Nietzsche contra Wagner* was put together) comes *Götzendämmerung*. In the autumn were produced the only finished part of *Der Wille zur Macht*—namely *Der Antichrist*—and the autobiography *Ecce homo*. None of these was published for some years, *Ecce homo* not until 1908.

Unquestionably the tone of these last works is unlike anything we have found before. Sweeping—one-sided if one will—though Nietzsche had been, fiercely though he had attacked institutions, ideas, and persons, his works had never been spoiled by the self-exaltation which we now observe, nor had he ever displayed such complete disregard of all beliefs and feelings from which he differed. Most of the offence which he has caused to reasonable people has been caused by the last works: and friendly or impartial critics can hardly avoid an angry regret that he ever allowed himself to indulge in these crudities. They do not help his purpose. Christianity, if it deserves to be overthrown, will not be overthrown by wild declamation, unsupported by argument, such as he employs in *Der Antichrist*. Other writers and other opinions cannot be routed by mere abuse, however cleverly epigrammatical,[1] such as occupies far too large a part of *Götzendämmerung*. Anyone who, like myself, is sceptical of the merits of Nietzscheism, cannot help feeling that these last works, *Der Wille zur Macht* excepted, only make his Weltanschauung seem less convincing and less reasonable. And, apart from that, he persuades us all the less. A statement or an opinion which we might be prepared to accept, which we should certainly be ready to consider on its merits, if it were presented in a reasonable manner, we feel strongly tempted to reject off-hand when it is thrust at us so stridently, partially, and uncritically as are the passages about early Christianity, Saint Paul, and so on, in *Der Antichrist*.

The causes, indeed, are not far to seek. All this unreasonableness, one-sidedness, and violence is explained by the intense loneliness under which Nietzsche has been suffering for many years. He finds that he has convinced no one: his friends have left him or, at the very least, have refused to follow him on his speculative flights. The critics are hostile or contemptuous. The followers, or disciples, for whom he longed, do not come. His health remains poor. And so, confronted with ever-increasing difficulties and burdens, he loses his self-control, and makes statements which are partly designed to outrage opinion, but partly unconsciously exaggerated. Even so, the challenge produced no answer; and the difficulties were actually increased by the means he had taken to end them. Not until 1888 was there any sign of interest in the outside world. Then Brandes of Copenhagen, who had been in correspondence with Nietzsche for some time, and had made a particularly careful and sympathetic study of his work, began lecturing on his philosophy at that University. The lectures were an outstanding success, and with them a certain appreciation of Nietzsche's work (especially in the North) begins. The philosopher himself set much store by them, and was much encouraged, though when we find him

[1] Admiration for Nietzsche's epigrams has generally been much exaggerated: for though he often succeeds with this weapon, a large proportion of his efforts, both in verse and prose, are dismal failures.

(for instance in *Ecce homo*) saying that he now has his readers in every European country, except Germany, we know that he is wrong. There was no general interest in his work before 1890.

In January 1889, Nietzsche, while in Turin, had a stroke, which left him insane. At first his insanity took the form of delusions, the commonest that he was either Christ, or Dionysus, or both: then he relapsed into gradually increasing paralysis. He was brought back to his mother at Naumburg and cared for by her and by his sister until he died, on August 25, 1900. He was buried at Röcken. His illness has been the subject of much controversy and discussion, into which I do not propose to enter. His enemies have made use of it in order to brand him as a lifelong madman. This is no doubt ridiculous, and yet many people have always had his insanity at the back of their minds, when reflecting on the value of his philosophy. I think that this is unjust, for impartial critical study of Nietzsche's work reveals nothing that we can properly call insanity or incipient insanity, until the last two years,[1] and I have already tried to account for the eccentricities of the last works. The strain, to which his last letters bear pathetic witness, is a sufficient reason for all the peculiarities of the last books. We do not need to explain them by arguing that Nietzsche was already insane.

Nietzsche's final Weltanschauung is more easily discernible in the unfinished masterpiece, *Der Wille zur Macht*, than anywhere else. In no other book did he attempt to draw up a system, or to emphasise the various sides of his thought in their proper proportions. Let us briefly run over its main features.

In the first place, life is reducible to "Will to Power". The evolutionists, who talked about the struggle to live, Spencer who defined life as activity, were all wrong, all incomplete, because they were not clear-headed or courageous enough to see a little farther. Life is only very seldom a struggle for existence: as a rule it is a struggle to increase

[1] And even then, nothing in *Der Wille zur Macht*.

power. The "Will to Power" takes an infinite variety of forms, and lies beneath every activity of every living thing on earth. To what end? To none. "Wille zur Macht" is Good "an sich", not because it leads to anything. There is no design, no plan, and no morality behind the cosmos, no arrangement whatsoever, no God, no soul, no "real existence". "The real existence is that which we observe through our senses; nothing at all beyond that."

In the second place, everything recurs for ever in identical cycles. Put forward in *Zarathustra* on the grounds of ethical desirability, this theory is supported by a sort of mathematical and logical reasoning in *Der Wille zur Macht*.

Thirdly, because of the overmastering "Will to Power" (but partly also on grounds of general desirability, and of historical fact) no ethical code has any validity. Morality has never been anything but a weapon in the hand of those who had the will to gain power, various systems suiting various types and ends. We may finally divide all ethical systems into "Herren-moral" and "Sklavenmoral"; and in the civilisation of the future both will have their place. The former, based on the right of the strong man to do as seems good to him, will be the morality of the rulers; the latter, of which Christian ethics is the most perfect example, will be valid and binding for the masses, who only exist in order to serve and to obey. But let no one imagine that any moral code can have universal validity.

Fourthly, the evolution of man, physically, mentally, and aesthetically, has not nearly reached its end. Man must develop to Superman. This development must be the aim of all future civilisation and thought. When the summit has been reached, the recurrence of the cycle will necessitate the same evolution again.

Finally, all this is summed up, in the words of Nietzsche's first book, as "Die Philosophie des Dionysos". The Greek god symbolises the ideal type of man, and his worship sym-bolises the life which is to be desired. We find that Nietzsche really ends by teaching that which he had first put forward in *Die Geburt der Tragödie*, in a far more detailed, far-reaching,

and logical form, applied, not to art, but to life. All these
fundamental tenets of his final philosophy are most strikingly
and intimately connected with Greek thought and literature.

Before we conclude our brief examination of Nietzsche's
background, it would be well to say a few words about his
personality. He reveals himself to a great extent in his work.
This is only natural, since his life, from quite an early stage,
was philosophy. His supreme and continual interest was the
putting of problems, and their solution: though it is a fair
criticism that he was better able to put than to solve them.
That too was partly because he could not discuss them with
anyone. "I have entirely and absolutely lost the power of
judging my work, because I associate too little with men, and
read no books":[1] he said in a letter, as early as 1879. Later
on that difficulty grew far more pronounced. Nietzsche was
in most respects very unlike the ideal man or Superman of his
books. He was of a mild, kind, gentle disposition,[2] with a
great capacity for giving admiration. Yet his life was an
excellent example of his precepts, in the steadiness with
which he kept to a course when he was convinced it was the
right one, and in the ruthlessness with which he was prepared
to sacrifice friendships and happiness in the cause of what
he believed to be truth. He said in his last years that Wagner's
friendship, which he had unhesitatingly sacrificed to another
ideal, had given him the only period of real happiness which
he had ever known. In his constant struggle with pain and
illness there is also something really heroic. He was a complicated personality as well as a complicated writer. As a
philosopher he discusses nearly every side of life, except
Natural Science; and his talents are not only philosophical
and artistic, but, in an unusual way, religious. Though he was
such a violent opponent of religion, he yet had a deeply
religious nature. He says so plainly in some of his remarks
about the priestly orders and the priestly character; and his

---

[1] But his reading was, or had been, immense, and most varied.
[2] Though often irritable, and not easy to associate with for any
length of time.

respect for the priest as a type shows, as he admitted, how near to him he felt that he was. He began as a philologist. Then he abandoned philology as a career, but retained what it had taught him. Like Goethe, "the last German for whom I have any respect", he pursued an ideal which was a re-shaping or a revival of a part of Greek civilisation. That we shall see more plainly when we examine some aspects of his work in greater detail: but here and now let it be said that one cannot understand him unless one understands the influence of the classics upon him. His object in writing was to help men, whom he saw travelling on a road which led nowhere. That he himself was made happier by his problems there is no reason to suppose: but his unhappiness was rather due to failure and loneliness than to the nature of his thoughts. Those near to him, like his mother, he advised not to read his works, since they would only cause them pain or disturbance.

Every deep thinker is more afraid of being understood than of being misunderstood. From the latter perhaps his vanity suffers; but from the former his heart, his sympathy, which always says: "Ah, why do you want to make things as difficult for you as they are for me?"

CHAPTER III

Nietzsche and Early Greece

THE Weimar classicists knew little about the Greece of the sixth and earlier centuries. They are interested in fifth-century culture, in the Periclean age, and particularly in the later Periclean age. They admire and they take for their inspiration works of art which are a little too late, or even slightly degenerate. The young Winckelmann is strongly attracted by Xenophon, and the mature Winckelmann bases his criticism of Greek art upon late, often very late, pieces, as he was bound to do, since few of the older works were then accessible. Goethe and Schiller seldom speak about Greek literature before Aeschylus, save only for Homer—who at nearly all periods of Greek study has been a "classic"—and actually it is Euripides whose tragedy most affected their own work. This concentration of interest upon the fifth century (there have been, and still are, excellent reasons for it) persisted unchallenged for nearly half a century after Goethe's death, and still persists, at any rate in some quarters, to-day: but to-day it is not unchallenged: and many, if not all, of the best scholars consider it mistaken. There has for many years been a tendency, not to decry the greatness of Periclean Athens, but to protest that some of the older things are still better. Homer's fame has not suffered, but it does not rest to-day upon the grounds which appealed to 1780. Aeschylus is thought to be a better poet than Sophocles and Euripides, if not a more perfect artist. The poetry of Pindar and of the sixth century appears more sincere, if less polished, than that of 470 B.C.; and almost everyone agrees that the best, though not the most perfect, achievements of the Greeks in sculpture and architecture were passed by 450, just as the twentieth-century critic considers Winckelmann's beloved Raffael to be a little full-blown. The first man to hold

—or at any rate to propagate—such views was Nietzsche, and the modern view of Greece is in great measure derived from his criticism.

This attitude of Nietzsche to the different ages of Greek civilisation is already very noticeable in *Die Geburt der Tragödie* —indeed it is, like the description of the "Dionysus phenomenon", one of the most striking things in the book—but Nietzsche actually took up his attitude some time before *Die Geburt der Tragödie* was written.[1] He continued to think in the same way, except during his second period, to the end of his life.

Nietzsche's golden age is nearly always the sixth century B.C. It is over by the time of the Persian wars, after which (he says) Greece definitely begins to degenerate. But Nietzsche is startlingly inconsistent. Sometimes the Periclean age is included in the ideal period, with the Pericleans, so to speak, in a minority. "That which is essentially Greek", he says— let us note how he defines it—"which as Homer, Pindar, and Aeschylus, as Phidias, as Pericles; as the Pythian oracle and Dionysus, as the deepest depth and the highest height, is assured of our astonished adoration." So that "that which is essentially Greek", even where it is allowed to include Pericles, includes no one but him, from his own period, out of seven names which are mentioned together. So again: "The fifth and sixth centuries are to be discovered now; for that is the time in which Greek life reached its height". But as a matter of fact Nietzsche does not usually include Pericles, nor any of Pericles' contemporaries, nor anyone later than Aeschylus, among his "greatest Greeks". He ordinarily only allows such a title to the men of the sixth century. "It is our purpose to release the sixth century from its grave. The sixth century is the summit."

As I have said, this is nothing unusual to-day: but it was revolutionary then; and we immediately want to see (1) on what grounds Nietzsche justified these opinions, and (2) how

---

[1] The earliest traces of such a thing which I can discover are in a school essay from the year 1861, concerning Hölderlin, and especially Hölderlin's *Empedocles*.

he came to hold them. Did any contemporary influences lead him in that direction, or was he simply following an impulse of his own spirit? The latter question will entail some examination of the philology and the influences of Nietzsche's early years, the former can be answered without preliminaries.

From first to last—even in his second period—Nietzsche is above all else concerned with the question of culture: and his opinions as to what constitutes culture have, from his first utterance, their characteristic stamp, so unlike the prevalent standards of his time. And as he is sceptical (to put it mildly) about the merits of contemporary German culture, so he is sceptical about the period of Greek culture which was then usually considered the highest. And for much the same reason—namely, that the only sort of culture worth having aims at the production of the great man, of the genius. Such a period was the sixth century, but such was not the Periclean, far less his own, age. The earlier Greek era was the most naïve, natural, and great, the "primitive world of early Greece" provides all the best models for a future culture. The period was the age *par excellence* of Dionysus-worship, the age of warfare, tyrants, and music, and moreover, unlike Periclean Athens, it had "a horizon encircled by myths". Therefore it was one of those rare epochs which could possess and bring to fruition its sound creative natural power, and "enclose and unify a whole movement in culture". (We remember that one of the great reasons for damning contemporary German civilisation was that it entirely lacked unity, that it consisted in a mere confusion of all forms and ideas of culture.) "Only there, whither the beam of myth falls, does the life of the Greeks shine bright: everywhere else it is gloomy." And that is why Aeschylus is a greater artist than Euripides or (strange judgment for the 'seventies) Sophocles, because he is earlier, nearer to the myth and the mysteries. "Aeschylus conceals a height of the Greek spirit which dies out with him...the best time and the highest point of the Greek musical drama is Aeschylus in his first great period, before he was yet influenced by Sophocles."

But the greatness of the sixth century bore no lasting fruits: from Aeschylus down to Nietzsche himself no single man has been its child, or recognised its beauty: in a few years—fifty at the most—Greece fell under the sway of a totally different set of ideas, a totally new scale of values—values which themselves degenerated, and led, by a logical and regrettable development, to the modern half-world.

Why? Because, in the first place, the Persian wars led to the political and intellectual supremacy of Athens:[1] and Athens (who had said this before Nietzsche?), Athens was not the state to develop the greatest tendencies of the Greeks: she replaced them, gradually, by her own peculiar characteristics, of which the most fatal was the tendency to speculate and to argue. The perfect (and ruinous) product of this tendency was Socrates,[2] who, more than any other individual, was responsible for the devastation of Europe. Socrates is the perfect example, as well as the first example, of "the theoretical man": that is to say, the man who will be, must be, is, anti-musical, anti-lyrical, anti-artistic, anti-Dionysiac, and anti-Greek. When we examine the grounds on which Socrates is to be condemned, we shall again see, by contrast, the grounds on which ancient Greece is to be admired. Socrates was the first reasoner, or at any rate the first who made reasoning popular, who inaugurated an age of reasoning. That was bad: but it was worse still that he condemned art, killed art, in order to put ethics in its stead. Of course, it is true that Plato, as in the *Republic*, does condemn art as harmful: but as a matter of fact he was not the first person to do so. Plutarch (*Solon*, chap. xxix) records that Solon disapproved of Thespis and his plays, *because he told such lies in them*. Presumably Solon, and quite likely many other *sixth-century*

[1] "The Persian wars were the national disaster: the success was too great, all the evil instincts broke loose, the tyrannical longing to dominate all Greece attacked individual men and cities. With the supremacy of Athens (on spiritual soil) a whole crowd of powers were suppressed...."

[2] Nietzsche hates and condemns Socrates in periods I and III of his work: in period II he speaks of him with respect and admiration.

Greeks, considered impersonation to be a form of false-hood.¹ So it seems as if the decline of Greece began before Socrates, that sixth-century Greece actually contained those elements which Nietzsche calls Socratic, and that Tragedy, from the very first, provoked opposition in the interest of morality.

However that may be, there is no doubt some truth in Nietzsche's saying that Socrates believed it to be his mission to "correct existence"; and it also seems true that his correction was largely destruction. Like Nietzsche, Socrates was largely a destroyer: he pulled down the old conceptions, the "ancient Greek view of life"; and put in place of it—what? Nietzsche says in brief, "an anti-civilisation", which has swayed the world ever since. It is difficult to agree with this: Socrates was probably an unsettling element rather than a creator: if he destroyed an old Weltanschauung he perhaps made no new one. If anyone really set up (and caused men to accept) standards of judgment at the time when the greatness of Greece started to decline, it was probably Plato rather than Socrates. But did Plato really do this? Did he get his own Weltanschauung accepted? It is, in truth, a characteristic of the world from about 400 B.C., until the time when Christianity took hold of it, that there are no settled standards (except the practical energies of early Rome), and no generally satisfying view of life, such as Nietzsche, probably with truth, ascribes to early Greece.

As for Plato, it is no doubt impossible to separate him definitively from Socrates. Nietzsche, at any rate, makes little

¹ ἀρχομένων δὲ τῶν περὶ Θέσπιν ἤδη τὴν τραγῳδίαν κινεῖν καὶ διὰ τὴν καινότητα τοὺς πολλοὺς ἄγοντος τοῦ πράγματος, οὔπω δ᾽ εἰς ἅμιλλαν ἐναγώνιον ἐξηγμένου, φύσει φιλήκοος ὢν καὶ φιλομαθὴς ὁ Σόλων.... ἐθεάσατο τὸν Θέσπιν αὐτὸν ὑποκρινόμενον, ὥσπερ ἔθος ἦν τοῖς παλαιοῖς, μετὰ δὲ τὴν θέαν προσαγορεύσας αὐτὸν ἠρώτησεν, εἰ τοσούτων ἐναντίον οὐκ αἰσχύνεται τηλικαῦτα ψευδόμενος· φήσαντος δὲ τοῦ Θεσπίδος μὴ δεινὸν εἶναι τὸ μετὰ παιδιᾶς λέγειν τὰ τοιαῦτα καὶ πράττειν, σφόδρα τῇ βακτηρίᾳ τὴν γῆν πατάξας ὁ Σόλων "τάχυ μέντοι τὴν παιδιάν" ἔφη "ταύτην ἐπαινοῦντες καὶ τιμῶντες εὑρήσομεν ἐν τοῖς συμβολαίοις." (Quoted by Professor Pickard-Cambridge, *Dithyramb, Tragedy, and Comedy*, p. 99.)

effort to do so; but both early in his career and late he evidently considers that the sayings and teachings of the Platonic dialogues are nearly all those of Socrates, not of Plato; and the criticisms he levels against Plato are in effect those brought against Socrates—anti-artist, hypocrite, moraliser—plus the special charge that Plato wrote extremely badly, and was, in fact, a bore. Only once does Nietzsche praise him, and that in a passage where he suggests that he might have been great, incomparably great, had he never come under Socrates' influence.

Of course Nietzsche, as usual, exaggerates the greatness of pre-Socratic Greece and depreciates the Periclean age: but there is no denying that much good recent criticism has virtually adopted his attitude: of course without the exaggerations. Many people at the present time would almost be willing to say, with Nietzsche, that *since* Socrates (but perhaps few would say *because* of Socrates) civilisation has really gone backwards. Nietzsche is entirely uncompromising about it, as he must be, since all his own constructive philosophy is built upon these premises:

The weakened Greek civilisation romanised, coarsened, grown decorative, then accepted as an ally by Christianity, as a decorative culture, spread abroad by force among uncivilised peoples—that is the history of Western culture. So much depends upon the development of Greek culture, since our whole Western world has got its impulses thence: fate willed that the later and degenerate Greek culture should show the greatest amount of historical force. . . .

No one will entirely agree with these and similar statements; but there is much truth, and much instinctive genius, in them.

But Nietzsche desired to be an influential, active reformer, from his first appearance as professor at Basel—or, rather, from the foundation of the "Germania" at Schulpforta—to the days when he endeavoured, feverishly and with no apparent success, to give the world a new practical philosophy of life: and the natural *practical* result of believing that sixth-century Greek civilisation was the highest summit yet attained by the human race would be—and with the (in some ways) practically minded Nietzsche, *was*—to try to return to it.

And this, I am convinced, he does: his own final active system is a re-hash, with additions and improvements of his own and of other men, such as Comte, Goethe and Kierkegaard, of pre-Socratic Greece, not necessarily as it was, but *as Nietzsche conceived it*. And the most detailed analysis of the way in which Nietzsche conceived pre-Socratic Greece will be obtained from an analysis of his conception of the pre-Socratic philosophers. Not only was Nietzsche directly influenced by these, or by some of them, over and over again throughout his life: but his general idea of early Greek civilisation is epitomised (or embodied) in his idea of the early philosophers. Just as the *philosophers* Socrates and Plato are the great enemies, the great decadents, so the sixth-century *philosophers* are the most perfect representatives of that highest, lost, but perhaps restorable civilisation.

The most important work of Nietzsche on early Greek philosophy is *Die Philosophie im tragischen Zeitalter der Griechen*. The thoughts expressed in this large fragment first suggested themselves to Nietzsche during his student years (there exists, for example, an interesting unfinished essay about Democritus, from the autumn of 1867), but in the main they were put down for the first time in a course of lectures delivered at Basel in the Winter Semester 1869–70; so that they are almost contemporary with *Die Geburt der Tragödie* (which was first put on paper "while the thunders of the battle of Wörth were passing over Europe"). These lectures were repeated in 1872, and during the following three years Nietzsche conceived various schemes for publishing them, all frustrated by his ill-health. In actual fact the work was terminated in 1873, with Anaxagoras. Nietzsche never touched it after 1879, when he dictated a short second Preface to it, desiring and causing it to be published as a fragment, since he then believed that he was dying. He did not die, but he became occupied with other schemes and left this unfinished.

Naturally an account of pre-Socratic philosophy by Nietzsche will not be that of an ordinary scholar: it will have neither the merits nor the defects of such a work. "Philosophia facta est, quae philologia fuit", ended the Basler Antrittsrede, and over and over again the young Nietzsche had decried the dull methods, and limited vision, of philologists, especially, indeed, of those who had busied themselves with "the hitherto so shabby and mummy-like history of Greek philosophy". So he must make the pre-Socratics live, as his contemporaries signally failed to do: by making them live he will show the world their real, sadly overshadowed greatness, and the splendour of their age. He begins, characteristically, with the question: "How can we get a real insight into the life of that age?" He answers his question as follows: "My way of giving an account of historical things is really to tell my own experiences as occasioned by past times and men.... Our literary historians are boring, because they force themselves to talk and to pass judgments about everything, where they have experienced nothing...". He himself, on the other hand, reads and interprets the ancient thinkers just as the Italians take up a piece of music, "drawing it into their own passion", and interpreting it purely personally. So he sings the melodies of the ancient thinkers "after them": "I know that behind all the cold words there moves a longing soul; I hear that soul sing, for my own soul sings, when it is moved".

The book was intended to be a sort of companion volume to *Die Geburt der Tragödie*—that one might guess, if there were no other evidence, from the title "Philosophy in the *tragic* era of the Greeks". But there is plenty of other evidence. From various fragments of the years 1869–73 we discover that Nietzsche then intended to write a series of studies, political, artistic, and philosophical, of Greece in its greatest days. *Die Geburt der Tragödie* contains most, if not all, of the proposed artistic criticism (as indeed it contains the seeds of almost all Nietzsche's later ideas, and of a vast amount of the artistic and literary criticism of all subsequent decades): but this work on the philosophers is simply "the Birth of Tragedy regarded from another side".

The problem, or at any rate the first problem, of *Die Geburt der Tragödie* is: "How the Greeks settled with pessimism; with

what they overcame it". The answer, as we know already, is
that they overcame pessimism, or forgot it, by the influence
of Dionysus-worship. The problem (if it can here be called a
problem) is: Do the philosophers of this period look on life
in the same way as the artists? That is to say, is their inspiration Dionysiac, and, therefore, are their deepest beliefs
pessimistic? Nietzsche concludes—or, to speak more accurately, he is convinced from the beginning—that these
things are so.

> The types of the great tragic figures are the great contemporary
> men: the Aeschylean heroes have a relationship with Heraclitus....
> The thought of the Greeks in the tragic era is pessimistic or
> artificially optimistic....In the pre-Socratic philosophers as con-
> temporaries of Tragedy, as the men of the tragic era we find in a
> metastasis again the epic and lyric elements, all the requisites of
> Tragedy....The content of art and the content of the older philo-
> sophy coincide...the older philosophy is related to art, its view
> of life often let itself be inspired by art...an impulse similar to
> that which created Tragedy.

The truth of all this is exceedingly doubtful: indeed it is
most unlikely. The philosophic *value* of the pre-Socratics is
small: but that their speculations were in fact an effort to
attain some sort of scientifically plausible account of the
cosmos, no one, except Nietzsche, appears to doubt. That
there was very much mysticism in pre-Socratic philosophy is
quite clear: but, except perhaps Empedocles, not one of these
men seems to have been driven entirely, or even principally,
by mystical impulses. No doubt Nietzsche took up this
attitude because, in his perversity, he just wished to, not
because it was in accordance with the facts, if these were
impartially examined; for at this time (1869–73) science,
learning, scholarship were comparatively unimportant things
to him, and his ideals lay wholly in the sphere of tragic, that
is to say, Dionysiac, art. Nevertheless I do not doubt for a
minute that he really conceived the inspiration of the pre-
Socratics to be of this kind: had he not so conceived it, he
would not, at this particular epoch, have felt so closely akin
to them; for again and again he states, in the most positive

terms, that philosophy should be both a science and an art, "as was the philosophy of the early Greeks".

"Great perplexity, whether philosophy is an art or a science. It is an art in its aims...but the means to attain them, representation in concepts, it shares with science. It is a form of poetry...." The philosopher's description of nature consists in a mixing of poetry and perception, inextricably mingled, for the philosopher is a revelation of the workshop of nature, and like the artist he speaks of the secrets of that workshop: the impulse to gain knowledge, alone and uncontrolled, is a danger to society and to culture, and it is the duty of philosophy to see that the impulse is controlled and guided:

If we desire (says Nietzsche) to attain a true culture again, then unexampled artistic powers are necessary to break the unlimited impulse towards knowledge, to beget a unity again. The highest value of the philosopher shows itself in the places where he concentrates the unlimited impulse towards knowledge, and binds it into a unity.... So are the older Greek philosophers to be understood—they control the impulse towards knowledge.

Not only is philosophy, in general, fundamentally the same as art. Certain individual philosophers are singled out as being aesthetes and artists.

Only the aesthetic man regards the world as does Heraclitus...he has that contemplative pleasure in the world present before him, with which the artist looks upon his growing work...the spirit of Anaxagoras is that of an artist.... When I listened to the total sum of the music of the older Greek philosophy, I thought I heard tunes which I was accustomed to hear from Greek art, and especially from Tragedy....

So, then, early Greek philosophy and early Greek art are very closely connected—far more closely than anyone had yet supposed: indeed they are the same thing, seen from different sides; using different methods, they get the same results in their interpretation of life. The cosmos, *as it is*, is justified, so early Greek art and philosophy tell us: whatever life brings, we must accept in the spirit of the Dionysiac ecstatics. The philosophy of the early Greeks is the "philosophy of Dionysus".

I do not know (and I suppose that there is no way of telling for certain) whether Nietzsche derived his beliefs about Tragedy, and particularly his beliefs about Dionysiasm, from the study of the early Greek philosophers, or whether he conceived those beliefs out of his own head, and then applied them to the pre-Socratics: one or the other he must have done, for, as we have seen (and we shall have much more evidence of it yet), he continually couples the two together, from his very early stages. But Dionysus, and the ideas which are dependent on Dionysus, are the central point from which all Nietzsche's ultimate ideas radiate: if then Nietzsche had his conceptions of the pre-Socratics first, and derived his ideas about Dionysus from them, then all his final philosophy, and four-fifths of his influence upon Europe, can be traced back to what he found in pre-Socratic philosophy or, more accurately, what he thought he found there. If it is the other way round, it is an indication of the originality of Nietzsche's conceptions.

The sixth century B.C. is the strongest and healthiest period of Greek life. Had it not been strong and healthy, it could not have been the great tragic epoch, for tragedy is only possible in a race which is convinced, like the "older Hellenes"—like Hesiod, Mimnermus, Theognis, and all the poets before Sophocles—of the fundamental badness of things, but which is strong and brave enough to overcome, by accepting, this conviction. "Pleasure in tragedy is a mark of strong ages and characters." And in this, as in other things, the Greeks were lucky ("an unusually gifted, in a certain degree privileged people", Ritschl calls them[1]): their strength was at its height just at the time when they began to be philosophers, and they were therefore saved from the special dangers which the study of philosophy has for weakly nations, like the Germans. The Greeks began *their* philosophy "in happiness, in a ripe manhood, from the midst of the fiery serenity of their brave and victorious age of manhood...as the truly healthy they justify Philosophy". So then their opinion about anything, but especially about the value of

[1] In a letter to Nietzsche concerning *Die Geburt der Tragödie*.

existence, is worth far more than that of any modern, because they were masculine, self-confident, brave, strong, and untroubled by the doubts and weaknesses which beset and hamper modern speculators. A man like Empedocles, he says, can truly say what he thinks about existence, and it will always be important to know what his judgment was: "his judgment weighs very heavy, especially because he is not contradicted by any single different judgment of any other great philosopher of the same great period. He only speaks most clearly, but really—that is, if one opens one's ears a little, they all say the same".

The old philosophers are straightforward, sincere, naïve characters, not unbalanced by preconceived ideas of any kind, least of all by ethical prejudices; so they start in an excellent position from which to examine all sides of life accurately and clearly. Herein they are totally unlike the Socratic schools.

The goal of all the Socratic schools is a moral-goods-doctrine, that is to say, a sort of arithmetic and art of measuring in the ethical world. The whole older philosophy still belongs to the time of unbroken ethical instincts...with Socrates we get a search for the purely human ethics, resting on a basis of knowledge: it is sought for. With the earlier philosophers it was there, as a living breath.... Contrast of the pre-Socratics to the Socratics: their attitude to life is *naïve*.

So, too, later on: "As long as life is on the up-grade happiness is at the same time instinct....The demand for a reasoning virtue is not reasonable...a philosopher is compromised by such a demand". Therefore, because they have lost the powers of instinct, Plato and Socrates presage decadence. Socrates was "a cavern of all the evil desires, a monstrum in animo", a man who needed, more than other men, to keep his own instincts under rigorous control. Therefore, says Nietzsche, he made use of reason, of "cleverness, brightness, hardness, and logicalness as a weapon against the wildness of his instincts". Unfortunately he infected others with the same erroneous ideas, so that instinct decays altogether from his time on. "The great concepts 'good, just' are detached from the premises to which they belong...and then people look for a truth behind them, they are taken as

entities or as signs of entities: a world is invented, from which
they are supposed to emanate....In summa: the nonsense is
already on its summit at Plato's time." The next step was to
invent a type of man corresponding to this style of thought,
"the abstractly-perfect man, good, wise, just, a dialectician—
in a word the scarecrow of the ancient philosophers,...
Socrates is an impulse of the deepest perversity in the history
of values". Plato is just as bad. "He is in violent contrast to
all the deepest instincts of the Greek, he detached the instincts from the Polis, from the contests, from military
efficiency, from beauty and art, from the mysteries, from
belief in tradition and grandfather: he denied all the premises
of the 'distinguished Greek', the sterling type...he is deep,
passionate in everything that is anti-Hellenic".

All these things are in violent contrast to the admirable
beliefs of the older philosophers. All the instincts of the
early Greeks, says Nietzsche, were against such an argument
that Reason, Virtue, Happiness are identical.

> Then the great meaning in moral education was, that people en-
> deavoured to attain in this sphere the certainty of an instinct: so
> that neither the good intention nor the good means as such came
> first to consciousness. Just as the soldier drills, so was man meant
> to learn to act.

Therefore "the real philosophers are those before Socrates—
with Socrates something goes wrong".

But that is not quite all. The picture of the pre-Socratics
is not without any blemishes; because, though the pre-
Socratic philosophers belong to the good, strong, virile time,
they are not entirely free from the influences and signs of
decadence. For there had been a slight tendency towards
decadence even in their day. So they appear both as Reformers and as Conservatives. As Conservatives, when they
are struggling for what is genuinely, traditionally Hellenic
against those perversions which were just beginning; as
Reformers, in that they also endeavour to attain something
yet finer and more true.

> These philosophers show the vitality of that culture, which
> begets its own corrective...their efforts, though unknown to them,

are directed towards sanctification and purification in the mass; the mighty course of Greek culture shall not be held up, frightful dangers shall be cleared out of the way.

Parmenides and Democritus fight against the laziness of thought which is brought about by a wrong attitude to myth; Pythagoras, Empedocles, Anaximander inveigh against feeble satisfaction with life: Heraclitus against over-readiness to take part in society ("übertriebene Geselligkeit"); and so on. Every one of them is a traditionalist; and every one is also a reformer in some way, even if only in the greater reverence for truth and for discovery of real fact which they bring into the world.

It is an immeasurable loss that the reformation never took place. The Persian wars brought about the supremacy of the inartistic Athens. The great movements came to an end: all that remains is to write their epitaph. "The reformation of the Hellenes would have been a wonderful soil for the be-getting of geniuses, such as never yet existed....We have lost unspeakably there." The early Greeks, above all their philosophers, knew and said that the Great Man is the one and only true aim of human effort. Alas, says Nietzsche, the world had to wait for my teaching in order to hear that truth again.

The pre-Socratic philosophers are great *personalities*. In *Die Philosophie im tragischen Zeitalter der Griechen*, Nietzsche heavily emphasises the personal side, overmuch sometimes, so that he often falls into positive inaccuracy. He says plainly, in the two Introductions which he wrote for the book, that he selected those points which shed most light upon the personalities of the thinkers, for though the systems of these philosophers are now refuted,[1] yet " even the most discredited philosophies must contain *one* point, which cannot be refuted —such as a personal frame of mind, a personal colouring; from this one point one can acquire a clear picture of the philosopher". "There is in a philosopher something which

---

[1] This he would not have said even so little as five years later, when he reverts to a much more literal interpretation of the value of early Greece.

there can never be in a philosophy: namely, *the origin of many philosophers, the great man.*"

My description (he says) is a beginning, in order to win back those characters through comparison, and to create after their model, and once again to cause the polyphony of the Greek nature to resound: the task is, to bring to light that which we are always bound to love and revere, and that which cannot be taken from us by any later knowledge—*the great man.*

Even in the second period of his works, when he is pro-Socratic, scientific, anti-artistic, and, on the whole, quite out of sympathy with the feelings on which his reverence for the pre-Socratics was founded, Nietzsche says the same things about them, alone of all his former idols. In *Menschliches, Allzumenschliches* we find him saying: "And now let us honour the greatness of those Greeks who created science! Who among them tells the most heroic story of the human spirit?" In *Morgenröte* he says, in the same spirit: "I have made the acquaintance of no persons who inspired such reverence as the Greek philosophers", and again:

These are all *aristocratic* personages, standing aside from the people and from custom, travelled, serious to the point of gloom, with slow eyes, not foreign to affairs of state and diplomacy.... Nothing gives a higher conception of the Greek spirit, than this sudden fruitfulness in types, than this involuntary completeness in the erection of the great possibilities of the philosophical ideal.

Once, I repeat, we find Nietzsche saying that in Plato the Greek spirit might have attained yet greater heights, had Plato never known Socrates: but even while he utters such heresies Nietzsche feels nothing but admiration for the pre-Socratics.

The fifth and sixth centuries seem to promise even more and even higher things than they actually produced; but it got no farther than promising and foretelling. And yet there is hardly any heavier loss than the loss of a type, of a new, as yet undiscovered possibility of the philosophical life....There is here, as I have said, a gap, a breach in the development; some great misfortune must have happened, and the only statue by which one could have discovered the sense and aim of that great preliminary effort in the plastic arts, broke or failed: what actually happened has for ever remained a mystery of the workshop.

CHAPTER IV

The Philosophy of Dionysus

NIETZSCHE's first genuinely creative work, *Die Geburt der Tragödie*, centred in his discovery (or invention) of a new principle of ancient life, more splendid, though more terrible, than the qualities and beliefs ordinarily attributed to the Greeks, unnoticed, as yet, by any student, but unfolding the prospect of a new art, a new life, and a new salvation. This principle, the "Dionysiac" principle, said Nietzsche, was about to reappear in modern art, and to change the face of the world. On the second page of *Ecce homo*, which is one of his last finished books, we find a clear statement of his final *Weltanschauung*: "I am a disciple of the philosopher Dionysus". At the very end of the book resounds like a war-cry the question: "Have I been understood? *Dionysus against the Crucified*...". The appendix to *Ecce homo* consists of a number of poems, to which Nietzsche gave the title "Dionysos-Dithyramben". Shortly afterwards, when Nietzsche went mad, his most common delusions were that he was either Dionysus or Christ.

The conception of Dionysus, which finally took such hold on Nietzsche's mind,[1] had not always occupied him so much. Indeed, in the writings of his middle period, that is, after he had ceased to regard Wagner's music as Dionysiac, and had temporarily become a sceptic, very little is heard about it. Nearly everything that is to be found about Dionysus is either at the beginning or at the end, either before *Menschliches, Allzumenschliches* or after *Zarathustra*. Zarathustra is another name for Dionysus.

No one before Nietzsche had attached so much importance to Dionysus, the god of wine and of fertility, though all the

---

[1] *Ecce homo* is a later work than most of *Der Wille zur Macht*, where there is not so much talk about Dionysiasm as about other things.

facts about him (to which Nietzsche added nothing) were already widely known. His worship was orgiastic, derived from Asia, and performed at intervals with extraordinary and somewhat disgusting excesses of sexual promiscuity and savagery, such as are vividly described in the *Bacchae*. Dionysus was traditionally attended by the satyr half-gods and their chief, Silenus, and he was the lover of the forsaken Ariadne. Legend had it that he had been torn in pieces by the women of Thrace, and that he had risen again; and mystery rites, of which little is known for certain, were founded upon this martyrdom and resurrection. These rites were held to be of immense importance, well into the Christian era. Zosimus,[1] in the fifth century A.D., says that the Greeks believed that the whole human race was held together by the Eleusinian mysteries, though no one except Greeks could take part in them.

It seems possible that Nietzsche was started upon the course of thought which led him to *Die Geburt der Tragödie*, and thence, after some years, to *Zarathustra* and *Der Wille zur Macht*, by observing, and being impressed by, a very curious note which *now and then* is struck in Greek literature. The Greeks were the earliest enquirers in history. They learned more, and more accurately, about the world, than any other people were able to do for many hundreds of years; and they did so because, unlike their neighbours, *they were not afraid*. At least, if they were afraid, their fear was not so strong as their curiosity: and therefore they sailed the seas, and colonised, and beat the Persians, and philosophised, and argued, and lived a *rational life*. But every now and then their rationality, or their calm, or their curiosity, or their intellectual impulses, or whatever it was that dominated them, broke down, fled—for moments, not more—and in those moments it is revealed how much nearer the Greeks were to elemental, primitive, savage terrors (already in the sixth century half-forgotten, and therefore half-formless), than are educated or sceptical people to-day. In those moments something tells them that the gods are near them, watching them, *hostile to*

[1] See Bertram, p. 371 f.

them; if they are not very careful, they will give those jealous powers an opportunity to do them harm.

Little harm can be done to the poor man, who has nothing to lose, or the humble man, who feels himself poor, even if he is not: but vast harm can be done to the rich, the powerful, and the wise: they can be shattered by one blow from Heaven: and if they offend Heaven, the blow will come. They are certain to offend Heaven if they commit ὕβρις, that is, if they forget the true state of their helplessness, and grow arrogant, offensive, self-satisfied. For the great, it is doubly difficult not to offend Heaven, but doubly necessary. Words are dangerous (the Power *may* be listening, and hear them, and so be set free to act: this is a belief common to the super-stitious of all ages and races): wealth is dangerous: power is dangerous: knowledge is dangerous. "Stay", says Pindar, "for it is not always seemly to be present when pure truth showeth openly her face. Silence, I say, is often the wisest thing which the human spirit can devise." "I dare not say more", says Herodotus. "I know well, what it has to do with this or that, but I will not say it."

It is a feeling, I say again, which only occasionally comes to the surface: in some poets, of course, more frequently than in others: and I do not think it is justifiable to argue, merely on this, as Nietzsche argues, that the Greeks were, all and always, pessimistic about the universe. But there it is, lurking in the background, and occasionally giving tongue, this primitive fear; and it is precisely this fear which gives rise to that which Nietzsche calls the Dionysiac View of Life. There are three stages on the way to such a view of life. The first is a mere stirring of fear at the vague remoteness and half-felt hostility of a universe not made by men; the third is the full recognition of the terror, that is, its embodiment in a pessimistic philosophy: the intermediate stage is a sort of uneasy glance cast over the shoulder in the twilight—at what? That stage is represented in Greek poetry by words like those I have quoted; and the Greek poets seldom go any farther.

Nietzsche feels and understands all three stages, the vague

inkling, the cautious silence, and the truly pessimistic philosophy, the philosophy of Dionysus.

> "Be silent!"
> About great things—I see great things!—
> Shall a man keep silence
> Or speak great words....
> Speak great words, my enraptured Truth.[1]

That, though it is a late verse (1888), expresses the first stage. Silence—the first impulse: the second, speak great things, and the third, the heroic resolution, conquering the fear, because the fear is still only in its early stages, a mere hesitation.

But over and over again we find the second stage of the fear, when Nietzsche, like a Greek poet, suddenly knows that the celestial or infernal powers are, so to speak, waiting round the corner to catch the hated mortal if he makes a slip (such as an incautious boast, or *too deep a discovery*), and to destroy him. Utterances of this kind are strewn about all through his work, early and late.[2] In a letter of 1871 we find: "A word is a dangerous thing...how much dare one not utter: and fundamental religious and philosophical opinions are precisely the things of which one must be ashamed. They are the roots of our thinking and willing: therefore they ought not to be brought into the light". In *Götzendämmerung*: "Even the boldest of us has seldom the courage of that which he really knows"; and "Once for all, there are many things which I will *not know*. Wisdom sets limits even to knowledge". In *Der Wille zur Macht*: "Comprehension is an end"; in a fragment of the year 1872: "Humanity has in knowledge a splendid means to destruction....Every kind of culture begins with the veiling of a mass of things". In *Richard Wagner in Bayreuth*:

We, the disciples of resurrected Art, shall have the will to seriousness, to deep holy seriousness! The talk and uproar...about Art...we are now bound to feel as a shameless intrusiveness: everything binds us to silence, to a five years' Pythagorean silence....Who would not stand in need of purifying water, who would not hear

---

[1] A Dionysus-dithyramb.
[2] Most of the following passages are cited by Bertram.

the voice which adjures him: "Keep silence and be pure! Keep silence and be pure!" Only in so far as we are those who listen to this voice, shall we too participate in the great vision....

In the late preface to *Die fröhliche Wissenschaft*:

This will to truth, to "truth at any price", this young man's madness in the love of truth is spoiled for us: we are too experienced for it, too serious, too merry, too burnt, too deep....We do not believe any more that truth still remains truth if it is unveiled; we have lived long enough, to believe this...one should not see everything naked, not be present at everything, not wish to understand and "know" everything...one ought to pay more honour to the *shame* with which Nature hides herself behind riddles and bright-coloured uncertainties....Oh these Greeks! they understood how to live; for that it is necessary to keep boldly to the surface, the folds, the skin, to worship appearances, to believe in shapes, in sounds, in the whole Olympus of appearances! These Greeks were superficial—because they were deep!

This last extract leads us to the third stage of the elemental fear, namely its erection into a genuinely pessimistic, Dionysiac Weltanschauung: a thing seldom formulated in Greece: but hinted at, I should say, by a large number of utterances which are more precisely hopeless than the Pindaric and Herodotean sayings which I have quoted above.

ὄλβιος οὐδεὶς
ἀνθρώπων, ὁπόσους ἠέλιος καθορᾷ[1]

and

πάντων μὲν μὴ φῦναι ἐπιχθονίοισιν ἄριστον,
μηδ' ἐσιδεῖν αὐγὰς ὀξέος ἠελίου.
φύντα δ' ὅπως ὤκιστα πύλας Ἀΐδας περῆσαι,
καὶ κεῖσθαι πολλὴν γῆν ἐπαμησάμενον.[2]

So says Theognis, whom Nietzsche had so carefully studied just before he wrote *Die Geburt der Tragödie*: and so say nearly all the great Greek poets, at one time or another.

τὸ μὴ γενέσθαι κρεῖσσον ἢ φῦναι βρότοις[3]

[1] "No one of men is blessed, as many as the sun beholds."
[2] "Of all things the best for mortals is not to be born, nor to see the rays of the piercing sun. But, being born, to pass as swiftly as possible through the gates of Hades, and to lie covered with much earth."
[3] "For mortals not to be born is better than to be born."

runs a fragment of Euripides;

$$\sigma\kappa\iota\hat{\alpha}\varsigma\ \check{o}\nu\alpha\rho\ \check{\alpha}\nu\theta\rho\omega\pi\sigma\varsigma,^{1}$$

says Pindar; and Sophocles, the serene Sophocles, who "saw life steadily and saw it whole", has the most famous of all the expressions of Greek pessimism, in his

$$\mu\grave{\eta}\ \phi\hat{v}\nu\alpha\iota\ \tau\grave{o}\nu\ \check{\alpha}\pi\alpha\nu\tau\alpha\ \nu\iota\kappa\hat{\alpha}\ \lambda\acute{o}\gamma\sigma\nu\cdot\ \tau\grave{o}\ \delta',\ \grave{\epsilon}\pi\epsilon\grave{\iota}\ \phi\alpha\nu\hat{\eta},$$
$$\beta\hat{\eta}\nu\alpha\iota\ \kappa\epsilon\hat{\iota}\theta\epsilon\nu\ \check{o}\theta\epsilon\nu\pi\epsilon\rho\ \check{\eta}\kappa\epsilon\iota\ \pi\sigma\lambda\grave{v}\ \delta\epsilon\acute{v}\tau\epsilon\rho\sigma\nu\ \grave{\omega}\varsigma\ \tau\acute{\alpha}\chi\iota\sigma\tau\alpha.^{2}$$

And it is on this saying, or (to be strictly accurate) on a saying from a myth worded in exactly the same way, that Nietzsche founds his "Philosophy of Dionysus" in *Die Geburt der Tragödie*.

"Do not", he says, "believe that the splendour and beauty of Greek life, especially as shown to you in the Greek gods, means that the Greeks enjoyed life, if they reflected upon life's profoundest meaning."

Go not hence, but hear first, what the popular wisdom of the Greeks says about this same life, which spreads itself out here before thee with such inexplicable serenity. The old story runs, that King Midas hunted long in the forest after the wise Silenus, the companion of Dionysus, without catching him. When at last he fell into his hands, the king asks, what is the best and most desirable of all things for man. Rigid and immovable the daemon keeps silence; until at last, compelled by the king, he breaks out with screams of laughter into these words: "Wretched ephemeral generation, children of chance and of misery, why compellest thou me to tell thee that which it is most profitable for thee not to hear? The best thing of all is for thee quite unattainable: not to be born, not to be, to be nothing. But the second-best thing is for thee—soon to die".

And again:

There is a very ancient popular belief, belonging especially to Persia, that a wise magician can only be born of incest.... Yes, the myth seems to try to hint to us that wisdom, and above all Dionysiac wisdom, is an abomination odious to nature, that he who through his knowledge hurls nature into the chasm of destruction, has also to experience the dissolution of nature in himself. The sharp point of wisdom turns itself against the wise man; wisdom is a crime

---

[1] "Man is a dream of a shadow."

[2] "Not to be born is the best fate: but, if a man be born, then it is much the next best thing that he should return whence he came as quickly as he can."

against nature: such are the terrible words which the myth proclaims to us.... The best and highest things, in which men can participate, they attain through a sacrilege.

This explains what Nietzsche means by "eine dionysische Weltanschauung". It is an entirely pessimistic outlook on life, which sees at the root of existence things strange, terrible, and perhaps fatal. It sees that great wisdom only brings great disaster, that the more man knows, the more he will suffer, that the universe is not made or guided by a kindly or beneficent power. But it is a philosophy of acceptance. Seeing the evil, pain, and terror, the Dionysiac philosopher says "yes" to life *as it is*, not as optimistic religion or decorative art, the art of Apollo, represents it. From intoxication, the gift of Dionysus, the philosopher receives the strength to overcome and to accept, and in lyricism, intoxication, exaltation is the greatness of his creed—and the true greatness of man. In the belief that Wagner's music was an art of this kind, the only art of this kind since Greek drama, Nietzsche wrote *Die Geburt der Tragödie*; and when he discovered that his belief was mistaken, and that Wagner was growing more and more German and more and more Christian, till finally he wrote *Parzifal*, he turned away from him.

In his later years, Nietzsche felt that he had left *Die Geburt der Tragödie* a long way behind, and looking back upon it, like Goethe upon *Werther*, he was impelled to criticise the book with some violence—but with some truth. Actually these later criticisms are "sound and fury" rather than a damaging indictment: but it is as well to consider them briefly at this point, before discussing *Die Geburt der Tragödie* itself. They are mainly to be found in the preface which he wrote in 1886 for the edition which is now generally used, and in the chapter of *Ecce homo*, headed "Warum ich so gute Bücher schreibe".

In the preface, which he called "an attempt at self-criticism", he says that the original purpose of the book was *to give his ideas about the Greeks*, and particularly about "the serenity which is supposed to be found in the Greeks and in

Greek art". He had come to the conclusion, he says, that the Greeks were in reality a pessimistic race. But the ordinary term "pessimism" was not applicable to them, so he had gone a step farther, and put forward the idea of "Pessimismus der Stärke" (pessimism is to Nietzsche normally a sign of decadence, "of decay, degeneration, misbegottenness, of wearied and weakened instincts"). "What does the tragic myth mean, in the Greeks of the very best, strongest, bravest period?" Then he had carried his enquiry one stage farther. What was the true explanation of the phenomenon which caused the *death* of Tragedy, namely, "Socratism in Ethics, the dialectic methods, self-satisfaction, and serenity of the theoretical man"? Was not this phenomenon itself perhaps a sign of decadence? "Was the 'Greek serenity' of later Greek civilisation only the red of sunset?"

This was a new and peculiar problem. At that time the idea of Greek pessimism,[1] which to-day is widely accepted, had hardly occurred to anyone else; and it had certainly not seemed to anyone else that pessimism could have anything to do with Dionysus. But Nietzsche is, throughout, very positive, and absolutely convinced that he, unaided, has made an epoch-making discovery. Let us turn to the section in *Ecce homo*.

> I had discovered the only parallel and counterpart in all history to my innermost experience—and precisely by so doing I had been the first to comprehend the marvellous phenomenon of Diony-siasm. . . . I first saw the actual contrast: the degenerating instincts . . . (Christianity, the philosophy of Schopenhauer . . .) and a formula of the highest affirmation, born of fullness, of over-fullness, an affirmative answer, without reservation, to suffering itself, to guilt itself, to everything in existence that is questionable and strange. . . . Perception, the affirmative answer to reality, is just as much a necessity to the strong man as is to the weak man . . . an ideal.

He claims to have been, in *Die Geburt der Tragödie*, the first "psychologist of the Dionysiac phenomenon"; and at this late period (1888), he describes the book as "an account of how the Greeks got rid of pessimism—by what means they overcame it". From *Die Geburt der Tragödie* right up to

[1] Pessimistic: tending to look at the worst aspect of things, to believe that things tend to evil. Tragic: ending calamitously.

Götzendämmerung, he has kept (he says) consistently to the conception and the ideal, which he had been the first to set up, an ideal which in the later book he states once more in the following extremely enlightening passage:

The affirmative answer to life even in its strangest and hardest problems; the will to life, rejoicing, in the *sacrifice* of its highest types, at its own inexhaustible nature—*that* I called Dionysiac, that I understood as a bridge to the psychology of the *tragic* poet. *Not* in order to rid oneself of pity and fear, not in order to purge oneself of a dangerous emotion through an unrestrained release—Aristotle misunderstood it in this sense: but actually to be, far beyond pity and fear, the eternal joy of Becoming—that joy which also includes the joy in *Destroying*.

He continues: "In this sense I have the right to understand myself as the first tragic philosopher—that is to say, the extremest contrast and antipode of a pessimistic philosopher".[1]

He goes on to speak of the great hopes with which he wrote "the hope of a Dionysiac future of music", and of his utter disappointment. He tries (in *Ecce homo*) to cover up his disappointment by claiming that wherever, in *Die Geburt der Tragödie* or the *Unzeitgemässe Betrachtungen*, he spoke of Wagner, he was really thinking of himself. Most German critics seem to be convinced, and almost touched, by this explanation, which to my mind appears a little disingenuous. However, whether it is true or not, Nietzsche certainly did not abandon the Dionysus ideal in his disgust and disappoint-

[1] This cannot be allowed to pass without comment. Nietzsche says: (1) "I am a tragic philosopher, that is to say, the exact opposite of a pessimistic philosopher". The statement, as a general statement, may or may not be true (I think myself that it is not true): as a particular statement having reference to Nietzsche himself it is almost certainly not true: for it seems very likely that Nietzsche was in fact a pessimist (see separate discussion of this point, chap. VII). (2) "Greek Tragedy was tragic but not pessimistic." This again seems very unlikely. The overwhelming probability is that all the Greek poets, including the tragic dramatists, had a deeply pessimistic view of life, that is, they thought the world-order was bad, as bad as it could be. Nietzsche says: "Their natural tendency was to see things thus; but they overcame their pessimistic tendency by Dionysiac acceptance". But he is surely wrong.

ment over Wagner: for though we hear less of it in the books of his second period, he returned to it with almost greater enthusiasm in the last stages of his work.

So much for Nietzsche's later self-criticism. Let us now turn to *Die Geburt der Tragödie* itself, and analyse what he says there, bearing in mind, all the time, the fact that he subsequently disowned a good deal of it. He begins with the (at that time) challenging statement: "The development of art is bound up with the contrast of the Apolline and the Dionysiac". The art of Apollo is sculpture and the art of Dionysus is music. Normally these are in passive contrast or active opposition, but at intervals a reconciliation is established; and the most remarkable of such reconciliations resulted in Greek Tragedy.

The man who realises how frightful, how unbearable is the nature of all existence, will only be able to go on living if he has some powerful external support. The Greeks, the most naturally pessimistic of all races, saw, very early in their history, that this was so, and chose the usual means of combating this dreadful reality. They turned to Apolline art, the art which is similar in its effect to a dream (Apollo is the god of dreams). They created a mythical artistic world, the beautiful Olympian world of gods and heroes. They concentrated their minds upon the art of outward appearances, with its suggestion—fallacious but pleasing—of a world-order of similar beauty, meaning and symmetry. And in this way they distracted their attention from the unbearable depths and realities of life, or succeeded in forgetting its terrors.

So they lived; and while they were so living there broke upon them the other way of sustaining life, the religion of Dionysus. The symbol of Dionysus is not the Dream, but Intoxication, Ecstasy, Exaltation.

Either through the influence of the narcotic drink, about which all primeval men and peoples speak in songs, or at the mighty onset of Spring, which permeates all nature with desire, awake those Dionysiac stirrings, in whose climax all that is subjective vanishes in complete self-forgetfulness.... Not only, under the spell of Dionysiasm, is the bond between man and man joined up again: Nature too, alienated, hostile, or subjected, celebrates again her feast of reconciliation with her lost son, Man. Of its own free will the earth offers its gifts, and peaceably the beasts of prey of the rocks and the wilderness draw near. With flowers and garlands is the car of Dionysus loaded: under his yoke walk panther and tiger. Change Beethoven's triumphal Song of Joy into a picture, and be not behind-hand with your imagination, when the millions sink in awe into the dust: so you can approach Dionysiasm. [1] Now the slave is a free man, now are shattered all the rigid, hostile barriers, which need, whim, or insolent fashion has set up between men. Now, hearing the gospel of universal harmony, each feels himself not only united with his neighbour, reconciled, blended, but One, as if the veil of Maya were torn up, and only fluttered now in rags before the mysterious Original Unity. Singing and dancing, man expresses himself as member of a higher community: he has unlearnt walking and speaking, and is on the way to fly up into the air as he dances. Enchantment speaks from his gestures...he feels himself like a god, he himself moves now as enraptured and uplifted, just as in his dreams he saw the gods move. Man is no longer an artist, he has become a work of art: all the artistic powers of nature, to the highest ecstatic satisfaction of the Original Unity, reveal themselves here in the thrills of intoxication. The noblest clay, the most precious marble—man—is moulded and hewn here, and to the chisel-strokes of the Dionysiac maker of worlds resounds the cry of the

---

[1] It is interesting to note that Professor Korff sees just this sort of feeling prevalent in the eighteenth century, where, on first thoughts, one would be least inclined to look for it. He says in his *Geist der Goethezeit*, vol. II (Klassik), chap. II, pp. 34 and 35: "The dissolution of the limited Ego in something which is higher and ever more general: that is the essence of love, whose sway fills us with that deep-seated exultation which rings in our ears with the extravagance of rhetorical inspiration in Schiller's Hymn to Joy, and with overwhelming power from the last movement of the Ninth Symphony....This is the fundamental thought of this Hymn to Joy: that all happiness is an emergence from isolation, whether it be in the sense of active human love, or in the sense of loving absorption into nature—a spiritual union with the world, which is nothing other than a union with God. Of course this thought is not an original thought of Schiller, but the common property of the eighteenth century, and it is interesting that it occupies even Kant in his *Dreams of a Ghost-seer*". The idea seems to be mainly derived from the Pantheism of Spinoza, to whom Nietzsche gave a good deal of study: and it seems extremely likely that Nietzsche's "Dionysiac philosophy" is partly an adaptation of Spinoza to suit himself, just as the eighteenth century adapted him, and partly the result of a genuine influence or series of influences from Greece.

Eleusinian mysteries: "Ye bow down, millions? Dost thou suspect thy creator, O world?"

Dionysiac worship began in barbarian countries, where it was practised with a savage license shocking to the Greek mind. So at first it was kept out of Greece (says Nietzsche) by the power of Apollo, the triumph of whose art was Dorian architecture. Then, as the new cult gained strength and made converts, the two hostile deities had to come to terms. Actually they reached a compromise, so that the extreme manifestations[1] of Dionysiac orgiasm were never known in Greece. But the Dionysiac Weltanschauung swiftly replaced the Apolline. The religion of formal beauty could not satisfy the needs of this "people so uniquely capable of suffering". So Dionysus won.

The Muses of the arts of appearance grew pale in face of an art which in its intoxication spoke the truth; the wisdom of Silenus cried "Woe! Woe!" to the serene Olympians. The individual, with all his limitations and restraints, went under here in the self-forgetfulness of the Dionysiac state and forgot the Apolline precepts. Excess revealed itself as truth, contradiction, the ecstasy that is born of pain spoke of itself from the heart of nature. And so, everywhere where the Dionysiac penetrated, the Apolline had been superseded and destroyed.

In art the first effect was the replacement of the Apolline type of poetry, Epic, by Lyric. Homer is the typical Apolline poet: Archilochus is the typical Dionysiac poet. For a while the new type of art reigned undisputed, and we have the age of the great lyric poets, of the early philosophers, and the tyrants (who are "Dionysiac rulers"), the age of Greece which Nietzsche most admired. And in this age began Tragedy, emanating from the chorus, as the universal tradition had it, without (then, in 1870) being able to explain how or why. But Nietzsche sweeps aside all the previous hypotheses of the origin of the chorus, especially that of A. W. Schlegel, and argues, reasoning most brilliantly, that the chorus originally (and in *all* Greek Tragedy really) was

[1] This is probably not true. The Bacchae tore Pentheus to pieces, and the *Bacchae* no doubt is a picture of the normal excitements of Dionysus revellers.

the band of Dionysus' satyr followers; and that the tragic hero is really always Dionysus himself.[1] He even says that, during the whole period when Tragedy flourished, everyone realised perfectly clearly that this was so, so that Tragedy has a special importance hitherto unrecognised: for it is the artistic expression of the Dionysiac view of life. According to Nietzsche this means that it is a much more significant art-form than anyone had yet supposed. No man, he says, now and always, has found a higher philosophy of life than by recognising that the universe is incurably evil, full of cruelty, sorrow, suffering and injustice, so long as that man is also determined to accept all the evil, to say "yes" to life as it is, and to realise that there exists no moral order or divine justice. To such a man will be revealed the full significance of the Oedipus legend, which tells that the highest wisdom, the deepest insight into truth, so far from bringing happiness to the wise man or anyone else, is a sin against nature comparable to the sin of incest, and sure to meet with an appropriately dreadful punishment.

That is what *Die Geburt der Tragödie* has to say about the actual birth and principles of Tragedy. Nietzsche goes on to speak of the decline and ruin of this great art. Tragedy had reached its highest point when something of the Apolline element was added to it, when the original purely lyrical, dithyrambic form was reinforced, so to speak, by action and argument—only not too much argument. This stage is reached in the early plays of Aeschylus; and these are the best Greek tragedies. Aeschylus' later plays already show symptoms of degeneration, as the action and argument become more important (Αἰσχύλον σοφοκλείζοντα—Aeschylus writing like Sophocles) and Sophocles is well on the way to decadence, though the *Oedipus* is one of the best examples of Nietzsche's contention that terrific Dionysiac depths, as yet quite unsuspected, underlie the best-known myths.

He then examines the reasons for the decay and loss of the

---

[1] He is no doubt wrong in these details, but perfectly right in connecting Tragedy with Dionysus, which no one had done before him. That is his innovation and his great merit.

art. It had hitherto been something of an unsolved mystery why Tragedy so suddenly and so completely disappeared a few years after its finest period. Nietzsche attributes its disappearance to two persons. The first was Euripides, who introduced a new, false, argumentative, optimistic, decadent kind of work. The second, his ally, was Socrates. This point has already been discussed in Chapter II, and we need not dwell on it again.

So much for *Die Geburt der Tragödie*. Let us now see what Nietzsche has to say about Dionysiasm, Lyricism, Music in his later works. Let us take the relevant passages systematically, book by book, and see what can be made of them. We shall find that Nietzsche's interest in Dionysiasm is deep, constant and fruitful, and we may conclude that his ultimate Weltanschauung is in fact what he calls it, the "philosophy of Dionysus".

In the four *Unzeitgemässe Betrachtungen* there are very few references to "the ideas centring in Dionysus". Since these works are products of Nietzsche's pro-Wagner period, it is at first sight a little surprising that there is not more in them about the connection of Greek Tragedy with Wagner. But it is really quite simple, when we remember that only one of the four essays was devoted to Wagner himself, and that that one was written when Nietzsche was in a state of doubt and difficulty, immediately before his actual break with Wagner, though it is actually full of the highest praise. It is known that when Nietzsche was engaged in writing it, he was also engaged in making notes for his first anti-Wagner book, *Menschliches, Allzumenschliches*. The other three *Unzeitgemässe* are written in support of the ideals of Wagner and Schopenhauer, but they have not nearly so much direct connection with the basic ideas of *Die Geburt der Tragödie*. So we hear little about Dionysus in them.

But there are a few relevant passages. In *Schopenhauer als Erzieher* (p. 87 in the Musarion edition) Nietzsche speaks about the possibility—the necessity—of attaining optimism through pessimism. This is one of the essential things in Nietzsche's conception of Dionysus, and therefore one of the essential things in his own philosophy, though it is true that he does not say so in this place. But often he *did* say that in his young days he was a complete pessimist; a fact which is indeed perfectly clear from his early works. *Die Geburt der Tragödie* cannot by any stretch of imagination be called a work of optimism. The world did not appear to that writer as it appeared to Leibniz, the best possible world, but the worst. It is not until his last period, or possibly until *Die fröhliche Wissenschaft*, written under the stimulus of recovery from an illness that had lasted long and which at one time seemed as if it would be fatal, that Nietzsche writes, or seems to write, as an optimistic philosopher. Whether he is ever a true optimist, I doubt: but I propose to discuss that question in a separate chapter, and I will not anticipate. But however that may be, in reference to Nietzsche's late work, it is quite certain (one finds this over and over again in *Die Geburt der Tragödie* and in all the most important Dionysus passages in all Nietzsche's works) that the great merit of the Dionysus cult, as Nietzsche conceived it, was that it turned pessimism into optimism by fully revealing all the reasons for pessimism. Many times we find him saying that true optimism is *only* attainable in this way, and in fact that this is his own "tragic" optimism.

In *Richard Wagner in Bayreuth* we find Nietzsche repeating his contention, first made in *Die Geburt der Tragödie*, that the earliest dramatists were dithyramb dramatists; a belief which no doubt was wrong. In the same essay (pp. 262–3 of the Musarion edition) he speaks, not for the last time, about his desire to "Hellenise the world" and to "orientalise Hellenism". This is a striking and unusual thought, which has a close connection with Dionysus and his worship. For the Dionysiac cults originated in Asia, and retained many Asiatic characteristics. Nietzsche's likes and dislikes, in regard to Greece, are peculiar, and they seem to depend partly upon the presence of non-Greek elements in Greek civilisation. His favourite sixth century was more under the influence of the Asiatic world and more closely akin to it, than was the fifth. Dionysiasm itself is not a thing typically Greek,

certainly not typically Athenian, in its extremer manifestations: and I have no doubt whatever that therein lies some
of its charm for Nietzsche. Here he is so far carried away
by his idea of combining Hellenism and Orientalism as to
announce that it is the most important present task of philosophy. The ultimate aim of philosophy is "to simplify the
world".

In *Menschliches*, *Allzumenschliches*, part I, there is nothing
at all directly bearing upon this matter, and the philosopher-
god is not mentioned. This is what we should expect after the
disappointment of Nietzsche's Wagner enthusiasm, although
that only brought a temporary reaction against the Dionysus
ideal. But for the moment the reaction is complete and there
is nothing to be found even in the fragments, sketches, and
plans connected with the book. In the second part, "Der
Wanderer und sein Schatten", written, it may be noted, later
(in 1879) and originally intended as a separate work, there is
one sentence (aphorism 187) concerning the conception of
ioy in the ancient world, which might lead one to suppose that
Nietzsche was again thinking on the old lines; but it is not
possible to make very much of it. Similarly in *Morgenröte*
Nietzsche once more refers to the connection between
Tragedy and Music, which was one of the main points in
Die Geburt der Tragödie and one of the main arguments for
the association of tragedy with Dionysus. So again it looks
as if he is coming back to his earlier interests.

Die fröhliche Wissenschaft, though it too belongs to Nietzsche's pro-Socratic and anti-musical period, contains rather
more about Dionysiasm than the last two books. But that is
as one would expect; for Nietzsche is now outgrowing his
second stage, and is on the point of writing *Also sprach
Zarathustra*. There are at least three things which we must
briefly examine.

Two of them flatly contradict one another; and it is
possible that between them comes the true turning-point
from Nietzsche's second stage to his third. We remember
how *Die Geburt der Tragödie* spoke of tragedy and tragedy's
aim. Tragedy was the art of Dionysus, and expressed the

Dionysiac philosophy of life. In section 80 of *Die fröhliche Wissenschaft*, we find a totally different explanation.

The Greeks took the deep background away from Tragedy itself and dictated to it a law of fine speech; yes, altogether they did everything possible to counteract the elemental effect of scenes awakening pity and fear: *they did not want pity and fear....* The Athenian went to the theatre *in order to hear fine speeches*!...

But in aphorism 370, "Was ist Romantik?" we find *Die Geburt der Tragödie* revived. Nietzsche begins by explaining his former enthusiasm for Wagner.

It will perhaps be remembered...that in the beginning I set upon this modern world with a number of gross errors and over-valuations, and anyhow as a man full of hope. I understood the philosophical pessimism of the nineteenth century as if it were the symptom of higher power of thought, of rash bravery, of victorious fullness of life. In the same way I interpreted German music to suit myself as the expression of a Dionysiac greatness of the German soul....

He goes on to explain, even more clearly than he had in *Die Geburt der Tragödie*, what Dionysiasm is:

But there are sufferers of two kinds, in the first place those who suffer from the over-fullness of life, those who desire a Dionysiac art and similarly a tragic outlook and insight into life, and then those who suffer from the impoverishment of life....He who is most rich in fullness of life, the Dionysiac god and man, can not only permit himself to see what is frightful and questionable, but can even permit himself frightful actions and every luxury of destruction, disintegration, denial; where he is concerned, that which is evil, senseless, and ugly seems, so to speak, permitted, in consequence of an excess of creative, fructifying powers, which would be able to make a luxuriant land of fruit out of any desert.... The longing for destruction, change, growth, may be the expression of a power that is over-full and pregnant with the future (my term for it, as is known, is the word Dionysiac)....That there can exist a classical pessimism—this presentiment and vision belongs to me, undetachable from me, my proprium and ipsissimum: only that the word "classical" revolts my ears; it has become far too worn out, too round and unrecognisable: I call that pessimism of the future— for it is coming! I see it coming!—Dionysiac pessimism!

This is perfectly in accord with *Die Geburt der Tragödie*, but it betokens an increase in the influence of the Dionysiac idea upon Nietzsche's mind. When we consider the problem of Nietzsche's pessimism, we shall do well to remember this passage.

The third passage from *Die fröhliche Wissenschaft*—or rather from the volume which contains it—is the poem "Musik des Südens":

> Nun ward mir Alles noch zu Theil
> Was je mein Adler mir erschaute
>   —Ob manche Hoffnung schon vergraute—:
> Es sticht dein Klang mich wie ein Pfeil,
> Der Ohren und der Sinne Heil,
> Das mir vom Himmel niederthaute.
>
> Oh zög're nicht, nach südlichen Geländen,
> Glücksel'gen Inseln, griechischem Nymphen-Spiel
> Des Schiffs Begierde hinzuwenden—
> Kein Schiff fand je ein schön'res Ziel!

This is a very perfect poetical expression of the Dionysus feeling. The longing for that which is Greek, in life, and art, and music, reveals one of Nietzsche's profoundest ideals.

Also sprach Zarathustra is a Dionysiac book, and Zarathustra ("jener dionysische Unhold") is Dionysus-Nietzsche under another name. The name Dionysus never occurs in the four books of *Zarathustra*, but that fact makes no difference: the teachings of *Zarathustra* are the "philosophy of Dionysus", the Weltanschauung of the book, especially the Eternal Recurrence, the supreme acceptance to all infinity, of *all* that life brings, is the Weltanschauung which Nietzsche had explained at the beginning of *Die Geburt der Tragödie*. But the Dionysiasm of *Zarathustra* is implicit, never explicit: there are no passages which I can quote as special references: and it is best to pass for the moment to those last works which are after all expositions and elaborations of *Zarathustra*, and little else.

Of these late works *Jenseits von Gut und Böse* yields two valuable passages. In section 255 and the following pages, Nietzsche discusses the music of Wagner, and then his own conception of a southern, that is, a *Greek* spirit in music. He desires

a music which does not fade away, die out, grow pale at the sight of the blue voluptuous sea and the brightness of the Mediterranean sky...which could still assert itself before the brown sunset of the desert, whose soul is kindred with the palm and can be at home and roam amidst great beautiful lonely beasts of prey....

That is the music of Dionysus, and that is the home of Dionysus-worship. The Dionysiac worshippers in *Die Geburt der Tragödie* were inspired by such feelings and such surroundings. So was Nietzsche when he admired the music of Wagner: so he is now when he condemns Wagner, finding that he is the exact opposite of that which he had formerly seemed.

The second passage, from section 295, is the most important and most direct reference to Dionysus since *Die Geburt der Tragödie*. But no longer is Dionysus "that artistic deity of the Greeks". No longer is the realm of Dionysus in the historical past or the ideal future; but here and now Nietzsche has become, as he says, the pupil and follower of the god, or he actually feels himself identified with his master.

The genius of the heart (he says), as possessed by that great Hidden One, the tempter-god and born ratcatcher of consciences, whose voice can descend into the underworld of every soul, who does not say a word, does not look a look, in which there would not lie a consideration and fold of allurement, part of whose mastery it is that he knows how to *seem*...the genius of the heart, who causes the clumsy and over-hasty hand to hesitate and to take hold more delicately; who guesses at the hidden and forgotten treasure under grim ice and is a divining rod for every grain of gold...the genius of the heart, from whose touch every one goes away richer, not favoured and surprised, not blessed and oppressed as by another's bounty, but richer in himself, full of hopes, which have as yet no name...no lesser one namely than the god Dionysus, that great ambiguous tempter-god, to whom once, as you all know, I offered my first-fruits in all secrecy and reverence....In the meantime I learned much, all too much, more about the philosophy of this god, and, as I have said, face to face—I, the last disciple and initiate of the god Dionysus: and now at last I ought to have a right to begin to give you a taste of this philosophy.

And what does the philosophy of Dionysus teach? It teaches men to be "stronger, more wicked, and deeper: and also more beautiful": as he would have them himself, and as he conceived the Greeks to have been. Such is the teaching of *Also sprach Zarathustra*, concerning which one may say that there is hardly a sentiment in it, of which Theognis or Archilochus would have disapproved.

There is also much in *Der Fall Wagner*, as one would expect, which touches one side or another of this problem. The ideal which is expressed in the sayings: "music must be mediterranised...return to nature, health, serenity, youth, virtue!" is undoubtedly an ideal in consonance with Dionysiac principles. The same ideal leads him to admire the painting of Claude Lorrain; and it becomes more and more an essential part of his outlook. In these later years he very frequently contrasts North and South, as he contrasts Dionysus and Christ. He identifies Dionysus with the South and the East, with dry air and heat; and he certainly identifies Christianity and most of his favourite *bêtes noires* with the damp heavy atmosphere of northern Europe.

Dionysus is the god of music. Greek tragedy was born "out of the spirit of music". Nietzsche's enthusiasm for music (and for lyric poetry, which goes with music) died out, naturally, in his second period: though even in that second period the form of his writing is lyrical or rhapsodical, not scientific, and he gets none of his conclusions by logical reasoning. In his third period he is even more rhapsodical, illogical, lyrical, than in *Die Geburt der Tragödie*; and no less musical. He has changed his views on music.[1] He desires "die Musik des Südens", as he longs for "southern regions, fortunate islands, the play of Greek nymphs", and his ideal "Musik des Südens" is *Carmen*.[2] But the interest in music grows more and more compelling, though lavished upon the unworthiest of objects, and it was certainly for this reason that he felt himself obliged to take up arms against Wagner, not once, but twice.

The second book against Wagner is *Nietzsche contra Wagner*. This is not new or original, but a collection and reprint of

[1] He ends by preferring vocal music to instrumental. It is suggested that he was influenced in this by Jakob Burckhardt's lectures on Greek music.

[2] In *Ecce homo* there is a section about *Der Fall Wagner*; and here Nietzsche calls the "Musik des Südens" "the flute of Dionysus".

various things which Nietzsche had at one time or another said about Wagner. Chronologically the work comes after all those which remain for me to discuss, for it was the last complete thing which Nietzsche wrote, but it has such a close connection with *Der Fall Wagner* that it is well to treat them together. The section "Wir Antipoden", which is a reprint in an altered form of a part of *Die fröhliche Wissenschaft*, repeats that the Dionysiac worshippers and philosophers are

> those who suffer from the over-fullness of life, those who desire a Dionysiac art and similarly a tragic outlook and insight into life....He who is most rich in fullness of life, the Dionysiac god and man, can not only permit himself to see what is frightful and questionable, but can even permit himself frightful actions and every luxury of destruction, disintegration, denial; where he is concerned, that which is evil, senseless, and ugly seems, so to speak, permitted, as it seems permitted in nature, in consequence of an excess of creative, restorative powers, which is able to make a luxuriant land of fruit out of any desert....

Götzendämmerung, the next work, describes the religion of Dionysus as that "with a joyful and confident fatalism in the midst of the universe, in the belief that only that which is Individual is to be rejected, that in the whole everything ransoms and accepts itself—it is a religion which no longer denies". Nietzsche is here speaking about Goethe: what he says is just as true about himself; for though he calls himself the great "Nihilist" (and with reason, for there are few things which he does not long to overthrow) yet he accepts everything that comes to him, life as it is, "he denies no more".

The section of *Götzendämmerung*, "Was ich den Alten verdanke", sheds much light on this question as on several others, though it must be read with caution, for it is not always accurate. In it Nietzsche claims that he was the first to discover the real significance of the worship of Dionysus, and that he was the first who even took the subject seriously. The views of the typical philologist on this problem are those of the ridiculous Lobeck. He goes to some pains to attack Lobeck (perhaps unjustly). So Goethe, since he did not notice or understand orgiasm, did not understand the Greeks. (That is certainly true.) What was the meaning of orgiasm in Greek life? It was an expression, the greatest expression of the Greek "will to life", one of the deepest instincts of the national character, like "will to power".

What did the Hellene guarantee for himself with these mysteries? Eternal life, the eternal recurrence of life; the future promised and sanctified in the past; the triumphant "Yes" to life away and beyond death and change; true life as continued communal life through begetting, through the mysteries of sex.

Hence arose the great reverence which the Greeks paid to everything that had to do with sex, reproduction, birth, and so on. The pains of birth, childbearing (and then all pains) are made holy and splendid through the religion of Dionysus. Christianity unhallowed all these things.

So he conceived the religion of Dionysus, and from this conception he began to understand Tragedy:

The affirmative answer to life even in its strangest and hardest problems; the will to life, rejoicing, in the sacrifice of its highest types, at its own inexhaustible nature...not in order to rid oneself of pity and fear, not in order to purge oneself of a dangerous emotion through an unrestrained release,...but actually to be, far beyond pity and fear, the eternal joy of Becoming—that joy which also includes the joy in Destroying.

And this brings him back to the point from which he started, to *Die Geburt der Tragödie*, "my first revaluation of all values".

Der Antichrist, one-sidedly occupied with Nietzsche's ideas about Christianity, adds nothing to this. In *Ecce homo* there are many important passages, of which we have already examined the most important in connection with *Die Geburt der Tragödie*. But we should note now that in the section on *Zarathustra* (pp. 400 ff. in the Klassiker-Ausgabe) Nietzsche claims that this work is the *apotheosis of Dionysiasm*. "My conception 'Dionysiac' here became highest achievement: measured by it all the rest of human achievement appears poor and conditional."

Also sprach Zarathustra is Nietzsche's greatest work, and one of the greatest works of all literature: and it is also the only finished work which contains the whole (or the whole that is important) of Nietzsche's ultimate Weltanschauung.

So that if *Also sprach Zarathustra* is the apotheosis of the "philosophy of Dionysus", then the philosophy of Dionysus is proved to be the basis of all that Nietzsche eventually held to be true.

What reasons does Nietzsche bring forward in *Ecce homo*, to prove that *Zarathustra* is Dionysiac?

He quotes one of the most famous passages in *Zarathustra*, and comments on it most instructively. The passage and the comments are as follows:

The soul, which has the longest ladder and can descend most deep; the most spacious soul, which can most widely move and wander and rove in itself; the most inevitable, which hurls itself with joy into chance; the being soul, which *wishes* to turn into becoming, the having soul, which *wishes* to turn into willing and desiring; the soul which flees from itself, and overtakes itself in widest circles; the wisest soul, which exhorts folly most sweetly; the soul which loves itself most, in which all things have their flowing and their flowing-back and their high tide and low tide— *But that is the conception of Dionysus himself....* The psychological problem in the type of Zarathustra is, how he, who to an unheard of degree says "no", *acts* "no" to everything to which hitherto people said "yes", can nevertheless be the opposite of a negative spirit; how the spirit who bears the heaviest gifts of fate, an overwhelming load, can nevertheless be the lightest and most other-worldly (Zarathustra is a dancer), how he who has the hardest, the most fearful insight into reality, who has thought the most abysmal thought, nevertheless does not find in it any argument against existence, not even against its eternal recurrence—rather yet another reason *to be himself* the eternal "yes" to all things....*But that is the conception of Dionysus once more.*

And *Zarathustra* is written in Dionysiac, dithyrambic language, both in the prose and verse parts. The supremely dithyrambic passage (so Nietzsche says) is "Das Nachtlied":

It is night: now all the gushing springs speak louder. And my soul too is a gushing spring.

It is night: only now awake all the songs of lovers. And my soul too is the song of a lover.

Something unquenched, unquenchable is in me; it desires to break silence. A desire for love is in me; it speaks itself the language of love.

I am light: oh that I were night! But this is my loneliness, that I am girt about with light.

Oh that I were dark and of the night! How would I drink at the breasts of the light!

And ye too would I bless, ye little sparkling stars and glow-worms up above!—and be joyful because of your gifts of light.

But I live in my own light; I drink back into myself the flames which break out of me....

Many suns circle in empty space: to everything which is dark they speak with their light—to me they are silent.

Oh this is the enmity of the light against that which shines: pitilessly it goes on its course....

Ah, ice is around me; my hand burns itself on that which is icy! Ah, thirst is in me; it pines for your thirst!

It is night: ah, that I must be light! And thirst for that which is of the night! And loneliness!

It is night: now breaks my longing out of me like a stream—it makes me long for speech.

It is night: now all the gushing springs speak louder. And my soul too is a gushing spring.

It is night: now awake all the songs of lovers. And my soul too is the song of a lover.

"Nothing like this", says Nietzsche, "has ever been composed, felt, suffered: so suffers a god, a Dionysus." And finally: "For a Dionysiac task the hardness of the hammer, actual pleasure in destroying in a decisive way, is one of the necessary conditions. The imperative 'Grow hard!' the profoundest certainty that all creative men are hard, is the real mark of a Dionysiac nature".

These are the reasons which Nietzsche gives for saying that *Zarathustra* is Dionysiac, and though they are short, they leave little more to be said. After all, the deepest message of *Zarathustra* is the message of *Die Geburt der Tragödie* again, that life is hard and unrelenting and hostile, but that all its cruelties and harshnesses can be vanquished in one way, by courageous acceptance. That *Zarathustra* is a pessimistic book I firmly believe, and sometime I hope to show it. The conception which underlies its real pessimism and its superficial optimism is simply the view of life which Nietzsche had expounded in *Die Geburt der Tragödie*, believing it to be the Greek view of life.

Finally, we must look at what Nietzsche says about Dionysus in *Der Wille zur Macht*. Nietzsche set out in this work to expound, systematise, and argue the statements which he had put forward in a poetical and inspired form in

Zarathustra. Unfortunately, he never finished the book, so that, edited as a vast collection of notes and fragments, it is not easy to read, and often difficult to understand. It adds little that is new, but it explains and argues many of Nietzsche's earlier dogmatic statements, and for that alone it is very valuable. Of this nature are the passages which are concerned with Dionysus.

On p. 116 of the Klassiker-Ausgabe Nietzsche states his solution of the ultimate questions of philosophy:

my first solution: Dionysiac wisdom. Pleasure in the annihilation of him who is noblest and in the sight of his gradual progress to destruction: as pleasure in that which is coming, that which is future, which triumphs over that which is present, be it never so good. *Dionysiac: temporary identification with the principle of life* (Ecstasy of the martyr included)....

But the most important and most significant passages are the last paragraphs in the same edition:

The deception of Apollo: the permanence of beautiful form: the aristocratic legislation: "so shall it always be!" Dionysus: sensuality and cruelty. The past might be explained as enjoyment on the part of the begetting and destroying power, as a continual creation. The two types: Dionysus and the Crucified. To be ascertained: whether the typical religious man is a decadence-form...; but are we not then leaving out one type of the religious man, the *heathen*? Is not the heathen cult a form of thanksgiving and of saying "yes" to life? Would not its highest representative necessarily be an apologia and deification of life? Type of a well-endowed and ecstatically overflowing spirit! Type of a spirit which takes up into itself and *releases* the contradictions and questionable things of existence!

Here I place the *Dionysus* of the Greeks: the religious asseveration of life, of a whole, not a denied and halved life (typical—that the sexual act awakens deep, mysterious, reverential feelings).

Dionysus against the "Crucified": there you have the contrast. There is *no* difference in respect of the martyrdom—only it has another meaning. Life itself, its eternal fruitfulness and recurrence, has as its necessary condition torment, destruction, the will to annihilation. In the other case suffering, the "Crucified as the innocent", is reckoned as an argument against this life, as a formula of its condemnation. One can guess: the problem is that of the meaning of suffering: whether it is a Christian meaning or a tragic meaning. In the former case it is intended to be the way to a holy state of being: in the latter case the state of being is counted as holy enough to be able to justify a huge load of suffering in addition.

The tragic man says "yes" to even the sharpest suffering: he is strong, complete, deifier enough to do so; the Christian denies even the most blessed lot on earth: he is weak, poor, disinherited enough to suffer from life in any and every form. The God on the cross is a curse upon life, a pointer telling one to rescue oneself from it; Dionysus cut in pieces is a *promise* of life: it is for ever born again, and will ever again return from destruction.

And the last section in the book is the clearest of all statements of Nietzsche's Weltanschauung.

And do you know too, what "the world" is to me? Shall I show it to you in my mirror? The world: a monster of power, without beginning, without end, a firm, brazen sum of power...this my *Dionysiac* world eternally creating itself, eternally destroying itself, this mysterious world of doubled ecstasies, this my "Beyond Good and Evil" without a goal, unless a goal without will lies in the blessedness of the circle, unless a ring has good will to itself—do you want a *name* for this world? A solution for all its riddles? A light for you too, most hidden ones, most undismayed ones, most midnight ones? *This world is the Will to Power—and nothing more! And you yourselves are this Will to Power—and nothing more!*

So the "Dionysiac" interpretation of life never failed Nietzsche. Everything else which he saw at work in the world, Recurrence, Will to Power, and so on, is Dionysiac: it all rests upon the conceptions of the earliest days of *Die Geburt der Tragödie*, and all those conceptions go back to what Nietzsche had gathered from his reading of Theognis and Sophocles and Archilochus, that the world is a bad place, but we must face it boldly.

CHAPTER V

The Eternal Recurrence

However hard a man tries, he will never get anywhere. However well he does his work, he will have it to do again. However virtuous a Christian he has been, he will go on being miserable for ever and ever. But if he has been confident, and cheerful, and strong, reckless, ruthless, un-Christian, he has the magnificent prospect of an unending repetition of his successes. For the universe can only run one course. It has already run that course through an infinity of time, and it will go on through another infinity.

It is in *Zarathustra* that Nietzsche adopts Recurrence as part of his own system. He had often referred to the existence of this belief in the work of others, and had speculated, in a detached or academic manner, upon its merits. Then, though he had always looked on the idea with distaste, he suddenly took it up with enthusiasm, and made it an indispensable part of *Zarathustra*, and an important, though no longer indispensable, part of *Der Wille zur Macht*. It is an idea which one meets—often—in Greek philosophy, and it is known that Nietzsche saw it there: but it is not certain (though I suspect it) that the influence of the Greek philosophers caused Nietzsche, half against his will, to become a "Multiplicationist".[1]

Let us begin our study of Recurrence by looking at Nietzsche's early criticisms, and by noticing how and when he changes his tune.

In the third *Unzeitgemässe Betrachtung*, "Vom Nützen und Nachteil der Historie für das Leben", Nietzsche speaks ironically of the Pythagorean belief that the earth "begins its piece afresh every time after the fifth act". In *Die Philosophie*

[1] Nietzsche is as inconsistent as usual about Recurrence. He criticises the belief as it is found in Greek philosophy, and then later on he says that no one thought of such an idea before he himself did.

im tragischen Zeitalter der Griechen he mentions that Heraclitus and Anaximander agreed "on a destruction of the world which repeated itself periodically, and on a continually renewed emergence of another world from the all-destroying conflagration". His comments on this show that the idea genuinely shocked him at this time; though from the relics of his planned tragedy "Empedocles" it looks as if he had considered the possibility of the reincarnation of individuals. When, in *Zarathustra*, he asserts the necessity of Recurrence, and its association with the Superman, he has taken up the ideal of development for its own sake, development "an sich", one might say; and therefore he desires the cosmos to return to the bottom, when it has reached the highest possible summit, in order to go through the same development again.

Who can *desire* the recurrence of life? The great, strong, happy man, whose life is so valuable in his estimation, that a repetition and continually a fresh repetition will be a pleasant thought to him. To everyone else, to everything miserable, misbegotten, which only looks upon its own life with dissatisfaction and repugnance, the thought must be frightful.

In *Menschliches, Allzumenschliches*[1] there is one important passage, which has a resemblance to Nietzsche's later thoughts, in that he talks about the "wheel of existence turning". This suggests that he had been speculating about Recurrence, but no more.

Future in some centuries: economy of the earth, letting bad stocks die out, breeding of better, one language. Quite new conditions for man, even for a higher being.... It was not always so: *but the wheel has turned and goes on turning*.

In *Die fröhliche Wissenschaft*, which is now and then so similar to *Zarathustra*, there are more instances of this tendency of thought than in any earlier book. The most striking is the passage in which Nietzsche imagines a spirit whispering, in the silence of night, that perhaps everything may recur over and over again. "The eternal hour-glass of

[1] Nachlass 462.

existence is for ever turned round—and you with it, tiny speck of the dust." What will he answer?

Would you not throw yourself down, and gnash your teeth, and curse the spirit who spoke thus? Or have you ever experienced a tremendous moment, in which you would answer him: "You are a god, and never heard I anything more divine!" If that thought were to get power over you, it would change you, as you are, and perhaps crush you; the question, at each and every thing: "Do you desire this yet again and yet countless times?" would be the greatest weight that could lie on your actions! Or how satisfied would you have to become with yourself and your life, in order to desire nothing more than this last eternal confirmation and sanction?

That is the important point about Recurrence, now and always. If (says Nietzsche) a man is confident and strong and happy (in other words, if he is the kind of man that Nietzsche wants), he will want this his successful life to repeat itself *ad infinitum*; and therefore, so he argues, if a man knows that his life is going to repeat itself anyhow, he will do his best to make it successful; that is to say, he will make himself into the desirable sort of man. If he cannot or will not do this, the thought of Recurrence will be too much for him, and he and his like will die out. "Let us see", Nietzsche says, again in *la gaya scienza*, "how the thought, that something repeats itself, has worked up to now." He replies, that from the first moment when anyone begins to believe it is true, "every colour is changed, and there is another kind of history". "This thought will continually prevail more and more, *and those who do not believe in it are eventually bound to die out in accordance with their nature*." We should note that in these passages, as everywhere before *Zarathustra*, Nietzsche is merely speculating about the effects of belief in Recurrence, not advocating it.

There is nothing else before *Zarathustra*. In *Zarathustra* we find, suddenly but not altogether unexpectedly, that the idea of Recurrence has become the keystone of Nietzsche's work. *Zarathustra* and the ideals put forward in *Zarathustra*, Superman, "philosophy of Dionysus", "Will to Power", are unthinkable unless based upon the belief that the cosmos goes in identical cycles. It has already been shown that

Nietzsche conceived the religion of Dionysus to be a religion of absolute acceptance of all that life can bring. Eternal Recurrence, too, is "the highest formula of asseveration, which can be reached at all". The mysteries of Greece are "eternal life, the eternal recurrence of life"; and he himself is "the last disciple of the philosopher Dionysus—the teacher of eternal recurrence". The fourth section of *Der Wille zur Macht*, as planned, was to have been called "Dionysos, Philosophie der ewigen Wiederkehr". There is little doubt of the connection between the two ideas.

The same is true of the Superman and the "Will to Power". If it is anyhow desirable to make man "stronger, more wicked, deeper, and more beautiful", that is, to raise him to Superman, it is far more desirable if he is to recur again and again and to go through all the same stages of development. Conversely, it is all the more necessary to progress to the Superman, in order to breed a being great and strong and joyous enough to desire the infinite recurrence of his own life. It is necessary "to create a being, who can bear this doctrine". The only being who not only can bear but welcome it is the Superman. "Zarathustra tells from out of the happiness of the Superman the secret that everything returns." Mere belief in Eternal Recurrence will tend to produce the Superman and to get rid of the weak. Such a belief is

the great disciplining thought, a hammer in the hand of the mightiest man, with which he smashes degenerating and dying races, and thrusts them out of the way, in order to make space for a new ordering of life, or in order to give to that which is degenerate and desires to die out, a longing for its end.

And so on. It would be easy to produce passage after passage of this nature, but it is not necessary.[1] Two more will suffice. The men who will be able to endure and to welcome the thought are:

The strongest, the most moderate, those who do not need any extreme articles of belief, those who not only admit a good deal of chance and senselessness, but like it; those who can think of man

[1] Cf. *Jenseits von Gut und Böse*, section 56.

with a considerable moderation of his value, without thereby becoming small and weak: the richest in health, who are equal to most "malheurs", and are therefore not so frightened of those "malheurs"—men who are certain of their power, and who, with conscious pride, represent the highest attained power of humanity.

The other passage, from the end of the *Wille zur Macht* fragments, explains all the consequences of the idea, and summarises its importance.

Such an experimental philosophy, as I teach, tentatively anticipates even the possibilities of the most thorough-going Nihilism: by which I do not mean that it would remain stationary at a negation, at a "No", at the will to say "No". Rather it will go through as far as the very opposite—as far as a Dionysiac asseveration of the world, as it is, without reduction, exception, or selection—it desires the eternal *circular course*: the same things, the same logicality and illogicality of association. Highest state which a philosopher can reach: to stand Dionysiacally to existence: my formula for it is *amor fati*.

It is necessary, for this, to conceive the sides of existence which have hitherto been denied, not only as necessary, but as *desirable*: and not only as desirable in relation to the hitherto accepted sides (for instance as their complements or pre-conditions), but for their own sake, as the mightier, more fruitful, truer sides of existence, in which its will expresses itself more clearly.

It is similarly necessary to value less highly the side of existence which hitherto has alone been accepted; to comprehend, whence this acceptance originates and *how little it is applicable to a Dionysiac estimation of existence*: I extracted and understood that which really says "Yes" here (on the one side the instinct of the sufferers, on the other side the instinct of the herd, and that third instinct, that of the majority against the exceptions).

Therewith I guessed to what extent a stronger sort of man must necessarily devise for himself, in another direction, the *elevation* and magnification of man: *higher beings* as beyond good and evil, as beyond those values which cannot deny their origin from the sphere of suffering, of the herd, and of the majority—I sought for the onset of the inverted formation of ideals in history (the concepts "heathen", "classical", "noble", rediscovered and set up).

We ought also to notice that Recurrence provides the strongest of reasons for the alteration or abolition of all standards of values. Among the plans for *Der Wille zur Macht* we find the title "Philosophy of eternal recurrence. An attempt at revaluing all values". In the fragmentary notes for this section Nietzsche argues that belief in Recurrence is so severe a burden that it might bring extremely grave consequences were not all ethical ideas to be discarded. "The revaluation of all values is a means of bearing the thought...in order to bear the thought of Recurrence, one needs—freedom from moral ideas."

These passages, which are all taken from books later than *Zarathustra*, and mostly from *Der Wille zur Macht*, are chosen in order to bring to light the close connection between the idea of Recurrence and the other main points in Nietzsche's final philosophy. In *Zarathustra* Nietzsche makes no attempt to explain the idea, to prove its truth by argument, or to state systematically how it is related to anything else, though he shows by simile and poetry that it is a thought which will affect and change everything in man's life. He brings the idea forward in the third part of the book, having held it back in order that it may make the most effective appearance possible. This is necessary because, according to Nietzsche himself, it is the most important thing in the whole work.

The basal conception of the work, the thought of Eternal Recurrence, this highest formula of acceptance, which can be reached at all, belongs to August of the year 1881:[1] it was jotted down on a sheet of paper, with the title below: "6000 feet beyond man and time". I was walking on that day beside the lake of Silvaplana through the woods; close to a mighty upstanding pyramid-shaped rock not far from Surlei I made a halt. There this thought came to me.

This passage, which is from *Ecce homo*, seems to me to be especially important, for the following two reasons. In the first place, Nietzsche states here, once and for all, that Eternal Recurrence is the "Grundconception" of *Zarathustra*. In the second, he implies that the idea was an inspiration entirely his own. It is therefore one of the few passages which assert that Nietzsche was not led by Greek philosophy to believe in his theory of Recurrence, or which at any rate minimise the influence; and though I do not myself believe that the connection was so slight, I feel bound to comment upon this evidence.

[1] The third part of *Zarathustra* was written in January 1884.

The principal references in *Zarathustra* are, in the Klassiker-Ausgabe, pp. 228–34, 289, 317, 319 ff., 334 ff., 461 ff., 469 ff. The first passage, the most famous and most important, ought to be given in full. Zarathustra is climbing along a steep, wild mountain path, and with him goes his archenemy, "the spirit of heaviness, half dwarf, half mole". Him he exorcises with the thought of Eternal Recurrence, so that he can climb to the highest summits.

"Halt, dwarf!" said I. "I, or thou: but I am the stronger of us two: thou knowst not my abysmal thought! It thou couldst not bear!"

Then that happened, which made me lighter: for the dwarf sprang from my shoulder, the inquisitive one! And crouched himself down upon a stone before me. But there was a gateway just there, where we halted.

"See this gateway, dwarf!" I went on: "It has two faces. Two ways come together here: no one has yet travelled them to the end.

"This long lane back: it holds an eternity. And that long lane forwards—that is another eternity. They contradict each other, these ways; they actually run their heads together: and here, at this gateway, it is, that they come together. But the name of the gateway stands written above: 'Moment'.

"But whosoever went One of them further—and ever further and more distant: dost thou believe, dwarf, that these ways contradict each other eternally?"...

"See", I went on, "this moment! From this gateway 'Moment' runs a long eternal lane *backwards*: behind us lies an eternity.

"Must not all that *can* run of all things, once already have run this lane? Must not all that *can* happen of all things, once already have happened, have been done, have run by?

"And if everything has already been there: what thinkest thou, dwarf, of this moment? Must not this gateway too already—have been there?

"And are not all things firmly knotted together to such a degree, that this moment draws *all* coming things after it? *Therefore*—itself too?

"For that which *can* run of all things: into this long lane *forwards* too—must it run once again!—

"And this slow spider, which creeps in the moonshine, and this moonshine itself, and thou and I in the gateway, whispering together, whispering of eternal things—must we not all have been there already? and return and run in that other lane, forwards, in front of us, in that long awful lane—must we not eternally return?"

So I spoke, and ever more quietly: for I was afraid of my own thoughts and half-thoughts. Then, suddenly, I heard a dog *howl* close by.

Thereupon follows the scene of the shepherd and the adder, a symbolic representation of the Nietzschean truth that despondency, pessimism, and oppression can be cast out for ever by the man who has knowledge of Recurrence, and determination to remember it. "No more a shepherd", it ends, "no more a man—a creature changed, a creature transfigured, who *laughed*! Never yet on earth laughed a man, as *he* laughed."

We have already seen that Nietzsche felt himself akin or indebted to Heraclitus; and on his own confession, or half-confession, as we shall see presently, he may have derived the idea of Eternal Recurrence from him. Some further support for thinking this is afforded by two passages in *Zarathustra* which show Nietzsche thinking like Heraclitus. The first is as follows:

There it was too that I picked up the word "Superman" from the way, and discovered that man is something which must be surmounted—that man is a bridge and not an end: thinking himself blessed on account of his morning and his evening, as a way to new dawns: the Zarathustra-word *of the great midday*, and whatever else I hanged up over man, like second purple evening-glows.

The second passage has reference to a "year of existence", "ein Jahr des Seins", a phrase which sounds like an echo of the Greek μέγας ἐνιαυτός, which certainly occurs in connection with Heraclitus. It runs thus:

"Oh Zarathustra", said thereupon the beasts, "to such as think as we do all things themselves dance; a thing comes and stretches forth its hand and laughs and flees—and comes back.

"Everything goes, everything comes back; eternally rolls the wheel of existence. Everything dies, everything comes into flower again, *eternally runs the year of existence*.

"Everything breaks, everything is joined afresh; for ever builds itself the same house of existence. Everything parts, everything greets itself again; for ever remains true to itself the ring of existence."

Even in Zarathustra the thought of Eternal Recurrence can be oppressive:

Eternally he returns, the man of whom thou art weary, the little man....Naked had I once seen both, the greatest man and the smallest man: all too like one another—all too human even the greatest!

All too small the greatest—that was my satiety of man! And eternal recurrence even of the smallest! That was my satiety of all existence!

But even if it is an oppressive, saddening thought, which might naturally and easily lead a man to dejection and pessimism, it has its own peculiar greatness; and that greatness will gain the upper hand:

Sing and bubble over, oh Zarathustra, heal thy soul with new songs: that thou mayst bear thy great fate; which was never yet any man's fate!

For thy beasts know well, oh Zarathustra, who thou art and must become: see, *thou art* the teacher of Eternal *Recurrence*—that is now thy fate!

That thou must be the first to teach this teaching—how should not this great fate be also thy greatest danger and sickness!

See, we know what thou dost teach: that all things return for ever and we ourselves too, and that we have been there already countless times, and all things with us.

Thou dost teach that there is a Great Year of Becoming, a monster of a Great Year: that must always turn itself over afresh, like an hour-glass, in order that it may take its course and run out afresh: so that all these years are like each other, in the greatest things and also in the smallest things—so that we ourselves are like ourselves in each Great Year, in the greatest things and also in the smallest things.

And if thou shouldst now die, oh Zarathustra, see, we know too how thou wouldst speak then to thyself: but thy beasts beg thee not yet to die!

Thou wouldst speak and without trembling, rather breathing deeply for relief and joy: for a great weight and oppression would have been taken from thee, most patient one!

Now I die and vanish, wouldst thou say, and in a moment I am a nothing. Souls are as mortal as bodies.

But the knot of causes returns, in which I am ravelled—it will create me again! I myself belong to the causes of the Eternal Recurrence.

I come again, with this sun, with this earth, with this eagle, with this snake—*not* to a new life or better life or similar life: I come eternally again to this like and same life, in the greatest things and also in the smallest things, that I may teach again the Eternal

Recurrence of all things—that I may speak again the word of the great midday of the earth and of men, that I may again proclaim to men the Superman.

So, then, the thought of Eternal Recurrence is on balance an intoxicating thought, at least to Zarathustra and to anyone who, like Zarathustra, is strong and happy, who loves life and activity and work, and even the pains and sadnesses and worrying responsibilities which are inseparable from life's joys. Such is the type of man whom Nietzsche would see in possession of the earth, the Superman, the masterful and confident being who did not flourish in the nineteenth century: but such was not Nietzsche himself, though no doubt he longed to be, nor can one believe that Nietzsche desired an infinite repetition of his own miserable life. For while Zarathustra is an optimist, Nietzsche is a pessimist. Zarathustra is Dionysus, the worshipped: Nietzsche is the worshipper: and though they are now and then very near to one another, there is yet a great and unbridgeable gulf between them.

But *Zarathustra* is not about Nietzsche, but about his creation whose name it bears: unlike most of Nietzsche's books it is not personal experience, sentiment, prejudice, or reminiscence, but an astonishing objective creation, the fruit of inspiration, not reflection, and therefore it does not always mirror its author himself. Certainly not here, for the thought of the Eternal Reiteration of this life becomes more and more exciting, inspiring, intoxicating (as it naturally would to a Zarathustra or a Superman), as the book progresses. So we find at the end the most dithyrambic of all Nietzsche's utterances, all dealing with Recurrence, such as the chapter called "The seven seals, or the Yes-and-amen-song", with its refrain: "Oh how should I not be lustful for eternity and for the wedding ring of rings—the ring of recurrence!...For I love thee, oh eternity!" And as a climax we find the last section but one, "The drunken song": "Was that—life? Well then! Once more!" and the song: "Pleasure desires itself, desires eternity, desires recurrence, desires everything to be the same for ever".

O Mensch! Gieb Acht!
Was spricht die tiefe Mitternacht,
Ich schlief, ich schlief—,
Aus tiefem Traum bin ich erwacht:—
Die Welt ist tief,
Und tiefer als der Tag gedacht,
Tief ist ihr Weh,—
Lust—tiefer noch als Herzeleid:
Weh spricht: Vergeh!
Doch alle Lust will Ewigkeit,—
—will tiefe, tiefe Ewigkeit!

Before we go on to consider the scientific reasons which Nietzsche advances, chiefly in *Der Wille zur Macht*, in support of the idea—and before we turn to the similar points in Greek philosophy, and their possible influence upon Nietzsche, there are a few more short passages about the probable *effects* of believing in Recurrence, which it is well to give. They are mostly from fragments.

Man! Thy whole life, like an hour-glass, will be continually reversed and will continually run out—a great minute of time in between, until all the conditions, from which thou hast come into being, come together again in the circular course of the world. And then thou wilt find again every pain and every pleasure, and every friend and enemy, and every hope, and every error, and every blade of grass, and every gleam of the sun, the whole association of all things. This ring, in which thou art a grain, gleams ever again.

We have heard all this before: but this time we find Nietzsche claiming for it a rather curious effect, for which we are hardly prepared: namely:

a new great tolerance....Whatever each individual imagines, the other will let it stand....He to whom effort gives the highest feelings, let him exert effort; he to whom rest gives the highest feelings, let him rest; he to whom discipline, submission, obedience give the highest feelings, let him obey. Only let him become certain of that which gives him the highest feeling....It is a matter of eternity. [1]

But

determined hostility against everything and everyone who seeks to cast doubt on the value of life: against the obscurantists and

[1] All this seems to me to be totally out of keeping with what Nietzsche usually says; for he is as a rule fanatically intolerant. I suppose it must be left at that—just another inconsistency.

grumblers. These must be prevented from reproducing themselves! This life—thine eternal life!...The imprint of eternity upon *our* life. This thought contains more than all the religions which despised this life as fleeting and taught men to look away towards an undefined other life.

The remaining important references to Recurrence are almost all from the *Wille zur Macht*, and contain Nietzsche's *scientific* arguments, which, though ingenious, are of little value. Before we discuss these, let us turn for a moment to Greek philosophy.

The idea of an infinite and exact recurrence of everything is rarely found in European thought. In the modern world it seems to be exclusively Nietzsche's, for theories of evolution have always assumed a development in a more or less straight line, not in a circle. So curious is the theory, that Nietzsche's remarks in *Ecce homo*[1] about the way in which he conceived the idea before writing *Zarathustra* do not convince me. As a matter of fact he must have known that the idea is to be found in Greek philosophy. His statement about Heraclitus, quoted above,[2] is not explicit; but it leads one strongly to suspect he well knew that Recurrence is found there. Even his words in *Zarathustra*—"that it was necessary for thee to be *the first* to teach this doctrine—how should not this great fate also have been thy greatest danger and sickness!"— do not sufficiently prove any absolute originality, in view of the real peculiarity of the idea; especially if we also look at Greek philosophy, above all pre-Socratic philosophy, to see what the Greeks had to say on the subject.[3]

It is here necessary to distinguish between Eternal Recurrence—"die Wiederkunft des Gleichen"—and Reincarnation, which does not necessarily imply succeeding world periods. Indeed, even where there are world periods, Great Years, and so forth, it is not necessary that events should repeat themselves exactly. All these three ideas, exact Recurrence, Reincarnation, and "mere" Great Years, are found in Greek

[1] See above, p. 98.   [2] See above, p. 94.
[3] This subject has been ably and exhaustively treated by Oehler in *Nietzsche und die Vorsokratiker*, and I am largely following him here.

thought somewhere or other, and involved and acrimonious disputes have been waged over the passages concerned.

It is believed that the earliest reference to such a thought (one of the authorities for it is Nietzsche's friend Rohde) occurs in an ancient fragment of an Orphic hymn: "But often the same fathers and sons and noble wives and dear daughters are born in the halls of each other in alternate birthplaces", but it seems most probable that this only refers to Reincarnations within a single world period: and it is not in the Orphic mysteries, but in pre-Socratic philosophy proper, that the important evidence is to be found.

There is nothing before Anaximander: but apparently something of the sort was taught by him. At any rate it is testified over and over again that he believed in an infinity of universes, though it is an unsolved question, whether he gave them a simultaneous or consecutive existence.[1] He also believed in a universal destruction.[2] There are two passages[3] which seem to suggest that he believed that these universes followed one another.

From these, especially when they are read together, it seems permissible to argue that Anaximander believed in a succession of world periods. There are also at least three passages[4] which seem to argue that Anaximander's infinite worlds were coexistent, though it is not clear that this is the meaning of the third. More one cannot say, but there is enough to show that the idea can perhaps be traced back in some form to this philosopher, who died not later than 525 B.C.

There are many passages which show that Anaximenes and Diogenes of Apollonia, both of whom were deeply influenced by Anaximander, and carry on a tradition which comes from him, spoke of innumerable worlds, and of their destruction and rebirth "at certain fixed intervals of time".

[1] Cf. Cicero, *de Natura Deorum*, I, 10, 25, and Aetius, *de plac.* I, 7, 2.
[2] Simplicius *in* Arist. *Phys.* 24, 13; Aetius, *de plac.* I, 3, 3.
[3] Hippolyt. *Ref.* I, 6, 1; Plut. *Strom.* 2.
[4] Aetius, *de plac.* II, 1, 8; Simplicius *in* Arist. *Phys.* 1121, 5, and Augustine, *de civitate Dei*, VIII, 2.

This is all very vague still: but when we come to Heraclitus we find something more definite, though still not very definite. Let us remember, though, that Nietzsche persistently calls Heraclitus a predecessor and a kindred spirit; and let us not forget the two passages from *Zarathustra* (see above, p. 100), which seemed to echo Heraclitean thoughts. What has *Ecce homo* to add to this?

I have sought in vain for signs of tragic wisdom even among the *great* Greeks of philosophy, those of the two centuries before Socrates. A doubt remained behind with me over Heraclitus, in whose neighbourhood I feel altogether warmer and more well than anywhere else. The asseveration of passing away and of destroying, the decisive thing in a Dionysiac philosophy, the saying "yes" to contrast and war, the Becoming...in this I must in all circumstances recognise the thing most nearly related to me which has yet been thought. The doctrine of the "Eternal Recurrence", that is to say of the unconditional and eternally repeated circular course of all things—this doctrine of Zarathustra might finally have been taught already by Heraclitus too. At any rate the Stoa, which inherited almost all its fundamental conceptions from Heraclitus, has traces of it.

This is inexact; and it is probable that the inexactitude is intentional. Nietzsche must have known more than this about Heraclitus. *Ecce homo* is a notoriously inaccurate book in such matters; and in this passage Nietzsche is deliberately setting out to magnify his own originality, greatness, and "tragic wisdom". And if for that purpose he finds it necessary not to mention that he is indebted to this or that thinker for an idea, it cannot he helped: he must produce his desired effect. I do not mean that we can say quite definitely that on this occasion Nietzsche is cheating. However much we may suspect that, there is no proof of it. The only indication is in the wording of the last sentence but one: "this doctrine *might* ('könnte') finally have been taught already by Heraclitus too". It is so odd for Nietzsche to say that it *could* or *might* have been taught by Heraclitus. Such a form of words must imply that Nietzsche thought it possible or even probable, but that either there was no evidence in existence, or that he himself knew of none. And of course there *is* evidence about it: debatable, inconclusive evidence, but still evidence to be taken into account most carefully. And plenty of it. Not a single obscure fragment which even a learned German professor of classical philology (one moreover who had lectured and written about the early philosophers, and had made them the subject of especially careful and lengthy research) might have overlooked or forgotten, but a number of well-known and much-discussed passages, which Nietzsche must have known and must have reflected upon. So it certainly looks as if that "könnte" were disingenuous, and the subsequent sentence, about the Stoics, seems less ingenuous still. For whether Heraclitus did or did not believe in Recurrence, and whether he did or did not influence the Stoics (a more doubtful point than Nietzsche seems to think), there is absolutely no doubt that this school *did teach* (*a*) ἐκπύρωσις, the periodical destruction of the world by the fire which is its basis, (*b*) the Recurrence of the universe in identical cycles after each ἐκπύρωσις. I say that Nietzsche cannot have been ignorant of this, though he would have us think so: but though he may have adopted the theory of Recurrence under the influence of Heraclitus or the Pythagoreans, there is little reason to suppose that he was affected one way or the other by the Stoics, whom he rarely mentions, in comparison with the pre-Socratics, the Epicureans (who certainly did *not* teach Recurrence), or Socrates and Plato.

But let us go back to Heraclitus. What is all this interesting but inconclusive evidence in regard to him?

First of all, the Stoics *may* have taken the idea of the ἐκπύρωσις bodily from his teaching, or they may have interpreted or expanded his meaning into that, or again they may have taken up the idea independently or from some other source. Actually it is very likely that they got it from the Pythagoreans. For it is *possible*, though by no means certain, that Heraclitus actually did teach the doctrine of ἐκπύρωσις, even if some of his fragments, which might be taken in that sense, refer only to the destruction of individual objects by fire. This, for instance, seems to be the meaning of the famous "all things are an exchange for fire, and fire for all things, as are goods for gold and gold for goods"; and of the

reference in Aetius: "Heraclitus and Hippasus the Meta-
pontine say that fire is the origin of all things; for all things
originate out of fire and end in fire".

That Heraclitus taught a destruction of the *whole* cosmos
by fire is disputed, for example by Burnet; but there is a
strong ancient tradition that he did. He seems in the first
place to have held that the whole universe was eternally
living fire; and in the second place, that "according to certain
cycles of times" the universe arises from the ashes of a
conflagration. Simplicius[1] says: "and Heraclitus says indeed
that the universe is destroyed by fire at times, and that it
arises again from the fire according to certain cycles of
times".

The phrase "according to certain cycles of times" deserves
to be studied more carefully. It clearly means that Heraclitus
believed in a regular time-cycle according to which the
universe ran this course. Regularly every so many years it is
burnt up, and regularly after such and such an interval it
begins again. This is getting very near to Nietzsche's idea of
Recurrence; though it still does not seem to be a compelling
logical necessity that the course of each cycle shall be the
same, even though each cycle has a fixed length of years, and
each interval of non-being a fixed length of years. But it is
only one step—and not a long one, I think—to say that
things will so repeat themselves.

And of course Heraclitus may have taken that last step—
though no evidence survives to prove it. We do at least know
that he spoke about a period which he called a Great Year,
μέγας ἐνιαυτός. It is reasonable to surmise that a Great Year
is a cosmic age, the cycle of fixed length x solar years. The
references to the Great Year are in Censorinus and Aetius,
not in Heraclitus' own fragments, and curiously enough the
former gives the length of the μέγας ἐνιαυτός as 10,800 solar
years, the latter as 18,000. The discrepancy is rather surprising, but it is probably unimportant. More we do not
know: but our knowledge is at least enough to cast grave
suspicion upon the passage in *Ecce homo* concerning Hera-

[1] Arist. *de caelo*, 294, 4.

clitus and Recurrence; and I think we may reasonably conclude (a) that Nietzsche knew most or all of the passages which I have here quoted, (b) that he interpreted them as meaning that Heraclitus believed in succeeding cosmic periods, very possibly identical in their course, (c) that he did not wish to admit this.

Empedocles, in whom Nietzsche was also particularly interested, certainly spoke of an eternal sequence of universes coming into existence and passing away. The best evidence is in the longish fragment number 17. Both Plato (*Soph.* 242 D) and Aristotle (*Phys.* VIII, 1, 250 b 26) understood Empedocles as teaching (and specifically in this passage) a state of cosmic flux, the periodical creation and dissolution of the whole universe under the alternating supremacies of Love and Strife. In his cycle there are four periods: the Sphere, which is the absolute supremacy of Love; the change from Love to Strife; the absolute supremacy of Strife; and the return from Strife to Love, completing the cycle. The world as it actually is can only exist in the "mixed" second and fourth periods. Empedocles imagined that periods of quiescence intervened between those of change. In this he differed from Heraclitus and Anaximander.

A similar theory is to be found in the Atomists, "who say that there are limitless worlds, and that of them some are born and others are destroyed, and that there is always a creation going on".

None of this is precisely the same as the Nietzschean theory of the Eternal Recurrence of all things exactly as they were before. It is not certain that these philosophers supposed that succeeding world periods would differ from one another, but on the whole it seems probable.

But the idea of Eternal and Identical Recurrence is actually found in pre-Socratic philosophy, namely in the Pythagoreans. It is desirable to refer to two passages—the most important pieces of evidence which exist in the matter—which appear to establish this beyond doubt. In Simplicius we find a passage concerning the Peripatetic philosopher Eudemus, in which the latter is represented as discussing the view that time recurs as it has been before, that as the seasons recur, and the other natural phenomena of the world without, so things are again the same. "And if one were to believe the Pythagoreans", he goes on, "then I shall again stand before you lecturing and holding my staff, and you will again sit there as you are now, and all things will be just as they are now.... For (they say) all things will be the same, and therefore time will be too."

The second relevant passage, which occurs in Porphyrius, is a short remark: "but in addition to this (they say) that according to certain cycles the same things happen again as have happened before, and that literally nothing new exists".

We know from the passage in the second *Unzeitgemässe Betrachtung*, quoted above, that in 1873 Nietzsche was aware of this Pythagorean belief. It is conceivable, but not likely, that in 1881, when he wrote *Zarathustra*, he should have forgotten it. But that small reference is entirely incompatible with the claim which Nietzsche advances in *Zarathustra* and *Ecce homo*, that he was the first in all the world to teach the theory of Recurrence, and I myself find it very difficult not to believe that, for some obscure reason of his own, he is being insincere.

This exhausts the evidence that the pre-Socratics either did or did not believe in Recurrence, and we have already glanced at the teaching of the Stoics on this matter. The famous myth in the *Politicus* is on the same lines, but it is not an exact parallel to Nietzsche or the Pythagoreans. God created the world, and after setting it on its way, at first steered and accompanied it himself; but after a time let go the helm and withdrew into a high tower to watch it make its own way. Left to itself, the universe gradually began to go backward upon its course, when its forward motion was exhausted, and became more and more disorganised as it did so, until God intervened to prevent its complete destruction. He took up the helm again, and set it again upon a forward course. Thus the cycle began again, and so it continues, and will continue for ever. It is likely that Plato only meant this as a poetical allegory, but it shows how familiar to Greek thought were ideas of cyclic progress, and it is much the most famous passage about such subjects.

I have not come to many positive conclusions by thus examining the idea of Recurrence in Greek thought. I cannot establish or prove that any ancient philosophers, except the Pythagoreans and the Stoics, believed that the universe moves in identical cycles. I suspect that Heraclitus may have believed it also; and I am fairly sure that Nietzsche deliberately conceals some certainty or strong suspicion of his own when he speaks about Heraclitus and the Stoics and Recurrence together. That is to say, I think that he very likely did take the idea from Heraclitus,[1] or the Stoics—or the Pythagoreans. For he is virtually trapped over the Pythagoreans by that small admission in the second *Unzeitgemässe Betrachtung*, when (not foreseeing that he would one day wish to appear as the *originator* of the theory of Recurrence) he spoke contemptuously of the Pythagoreans who believed "that the earth begins its drama all over again after the fifth act". So his claim to have been the first to teach this theory is refuted, and it can even be seen that he must have known that it was not a true claim. And though it is of no special importance whether Nietzsche invented the idea himself, or adopted or adapted it from someone else, it is important that he has been found insincere on a specific point: for if he is insincere once, where it does not much matter, it is extremely probable that he will be insincere in other places where it does matter. And if so, the foundations will crumble, and his work will have to be revalued; for all critics have hitherto assumed that, sound or unsound, good or bad, mad or sane,

[1] Another passage which suggests a Heraclitean influence is found in *Der Wille zur Macht*. "All Becoming takes place in the repetition of a definite number of absolutely like states. . . . That all recurs is the extremest approach of a world of Becoming to that of Being: highest point of contemplation." The phrases "World of Becoming" and "all Becoming" are Heraclitean. Heraclitus ("everything flows and nothing remains") is always associated with the idea of Becoming, not Being: his world is continually coming into existence and passing away, never remaining the same.

Nietzsche was always sincere. And if he was not? Let us hasten on to our next investigation.

This next investigation—it is also the last in our chapter on Recurrence—concerns the scientific arguments in favour of the theory which Nietzsche was elaborating (they are not finished) in *Der Wille zur Macht*. These arguments are interesting, ingenious, and plausible, but they do not seem to be logical. They run as follows:[1]

(1) The theory that the world was created is inadmissible.

The world becomes, it passes away, but it has never begun to become and never ceased to pass away....The hypothesis of a created world must not trouble us for a moment. The conception "create" is to-day entirely undefinable, unable to be accomplished; only a word still, rudimentary, from the days of superstition....

(2) Equally inadmissible is the hypothesis that the cosmos itself can possess "the capacity of the divine creative power, of the endless power of change"; because this would postulate an inexhaustible and continuously increasing supply of energy, of which there is no sign. "The world, as force, must not be considered unbounded, for it cannot be so thought— we forbid ourselves the conception of an endless force as incompatible with the conception 'force'. So—the world lacks the capacity to be eternally renewed."

(3) Time, on the other hand, is unlimited. "The time in which the All exercises its force, is endless; that is to say, the force is for ever alike and for ever active." So the argument is based upon these two hypotheses, (a) that time is unlimited, (b) that energy is limited. It is as follows:

The number of the positions, alterations, combinations, and developments of the force is of course enormously great and in practice immeasurable, but also certainly definite and not endless....If the world may be conceived as a definite amount of force and as a definite number of force-centres—and every other conception remains indefinite and consequently unusable—it then follows thence, that it has to go through a calculable number of combinations in the great game of its existence. In an endless time every possible combination would have been reached at some time or other; more yet: it would have been reached countless times. And as between every combination and its next return all other

[1] *Der Wille zur Macht*, Klassiker-Ausgabe, §§ 684 ff.

combinations that are possible at all would necessarily have been gone through, and each of these combinations necessarily conditioned in the same order of sequence, then thereby a circular course of absolutely identical sequences would have been demonstrated: the world as a circular course, which has already repeated itself infinitely often and which goes on playing its game in infinitum....

It would be a great mistake—a mistake like those caused by our usual anthropomorphic proclivities—to argue that this unending process has any ethical tendency or any moral aim. It would be bad science to argue that it has any goal at all; for if the universe had such a goal, it must have been attained already. If it were possible for the universe to come to a standstill, it would have done so long ago.

Nietzsche means this (admittedly unfinished) argument quite seriously. He even believes that his reasoning is strictly and seriously *scientific*. But is it? Let us look at it carefully and sceptically, and see if it is logical, accurate, or true. We shall find that it is not.

Suppose we begin by granting the all-important hypotheses that there cannot have been a creation, and that time is endless. We then have to consider (1) whether we can legitimately say that energy is limited. If it is, then the number of possible "Kombinationen" is also finite; (2) whether, if this is so, these possible "Kombinationen" must recur indefinitely.

Nietzsche does not define the word "energy" ("Kraft"): but we will not quarrel with him for saying that the supply is finite. Even so, however, his conclusion does not follow. Another definition is badly needed, and Nietzsche does not give it. What is a "combination of circumstances" or an "event"? The number of possible "events" will depend on how much one secludes from a chain of causes and effects; and therefore the number of "events" or "combinations" can be arbitrarily altered.

Nor is there any logical necessity that "events" need recur, whatever the circumstances. Suppose one has a box containing four balls of different colours, blue, green, white, and red. One is going to take these out and put them back, one after another, without first looking to see which is which. Suppose that the first time one took out the blue, and put it back, and next the green, and after that the white, and last of all the red. There is no logical reason why one should ever take them out in that order again, however long one repeated the process, nor indeed any reason, apart from deliberate intention (which Nietzsche does not allow) why one particular ball should ever again be taken out. Of course there is a probability, which can be calculated, that it would so happen; and the longer the time spent upon the pastime, and the smaller the number of balls, the greater this chance would become. But there is, and there can be, no logical necessity at all.

And then "Infinity" and "The Infinite". Surely Nietzsche speaks too lightly and too assuredly? Space is no longer said to be "infinite": it is defined as "finite but boundless".[1] The term "infinite" appears indeed to have lost all meaning in the circumstances in which Nietzsche uses it. Infinity, it seems, is now simply defined as something bigger than the biggest number which you can think of. Therefore it seems that Nietzsche has no right to say, as he does, that time is infinite, even if we allow him to talk about time, as everyone did until since his day, as if it were something which there were no difficulty in understanding by intuition. It is doubtful, really, whether the statement "Time is infinite" means anything at all.

Anyway, what is time? No longer, it seems, an "ever-rolling stream", the speed of which is easily and satisfactorily measured by a clock; but the necessary fourth dimension of a world which is inexplicable in terms of three. Since Einstein, especially, it seems to have some peculiar characteristics. For instance, an observer who should be projected at an intense speed to a distant part of the universe and back, would find, when he returned, that according to his own reckoning he had not lived as long as the man who had stayed quietly at home had lived according to *his* own computation. Moreover, it appears that two things could happen in a different order in respect of two differently situated observers—a fact which

[1] See, for example, Professor A. S. Eddington, *The Nature of the Physical World*.

makes it impossible for Nietzsche to talk about "absolutely identical" events or "absolutely identical repetition".

And when Nietzsche says that the universe can never come to a standstill, he is making a statement which flatly contradicts a law which seems to be of supreme importance in modern physics—the law that disorganisation is continually increasing, so that in a measurable and predictable time the universe will have reached a state when nothing further can take place. Let us refer again to Professor Eddington.

The practical measure of the random element which can increase in the universe but can never decrease is called *entropy*....Entropy continually increases. We can, by isolating parts of the world and postulating rather idealised conditions in our problems, arrest the increase, but we cannot turn it into a decrease. That would involve something much worse than a violation of an ordinary law of Nature, namely, an improbable coincidence. The law that entropy always increases—the second law of thermodynamics—holds, I think, the supreme position among the laws of Nature. If someone points out to you that your pet theory of the universe is in disagreement with Maxwell's equation—then so much the worse for Maxwell's equation. If it is found to be contradicted by observation—well, these experimentalists do bungle things sometimes. But if your theory is found to be against the second law of thermodynamics I can give you no hope; there is nothing for it but to collapse in deepest humiliation....

Whoever wishes for a universe which can continue indefinitely in activity must lead a crusade against the second law of thermodynamics....At present we can see no way in which an attack on the second law of thermodynamics could possibly succeed....[1]

Nietzsche's argument does contradict this law, as it contradicts the theory of relativity, and therefore it seems that he must be wrong. Yet the inferior value of his arguments does not take from the interest of the Recurrence idea or from its importance in Nietzsche's work. We are led to think that he would have done well to steer clear of mathematics, but our respect for his poetical genius is not diminished. He brought to this curious and probably untenable idea a wealth of that almost religious enthusiasm which is characteristic of him; an enthusiasm which is often infectious and convincing, even when it does not deserve to convince.

[1] Professor A. S. Eddington, *op. cit.* pp. 74, 82.

It is conceivable that Nietzsche adopted Recurrence from those Greek philosophers in whose works he knew it existed, certain that he adopted it because he thought it a desirable belief for his social and cultural purposes, not because he was convinced that it was true, as a Kant or Leibniz would have to be convinced before he would incorporate an idea in his system. Then, having adopted the belief, he finds it even more valuable to him than he had at first expected: he is carried away by it, becomes enthralled or intoxicated. This personal experience convinces him that such a splendid, such an over-powering theory of life *must be true* as well as desirable: were it not true, it could not mean so much to him, could not appeal so intensely to his instincts. So it is true, and being true it must be capable of logical proof, when the time for logical proof comes. In *Der Wille zur Macht* the time comes. It is urgently necessary to justify Recurrence by reasoning, and so Nietzsche sketches (but does not finish) this argument, which is no argument and never could be, however long he might labour to complete it. But even so he is not satisfied. To the poet in him no reasoned argument could ever replace or improve upon instinctive convictions; and it is to such conviction that he returns, in one of his most poetical and most imaginative flights, the closing section of *Der Wille zur Macht*.

And know ye too, what "the world" is for me? Shall I show it to you in my mirror? This world: a monster of force, without beginning, without end, a firm, brazen quantity of force, which becomes neither greater nor less, which does not use itself up, but only changes itself, unchangeably great as a whole, a store without expenses and losses, but equally without increase, without takings, surrounded by the "void" as its boundary, not a thing that fades away or wastes, nor a thing endlessly extended, but inserted as a definite force into a definite space, and not a space which could anywhere be called "empty", but rather as a force everywhere, as an interplay of forces and force-waves at the same time one and many, piling itself up here and at the same time diminishing there, a sea of forces which storm upon each other and flood upon each other, eternally changing, eternally flowing back, with colossal years of recurrence, with an ebb and flow of its formations, spreading out from the simplest to the most manifold, back from the play of contradictions to the joy of harmony, affirming itself still in this equality of its paths and years, blessing itself as that which must eternally recur, as a Becoming, which knows no satiation, no weariness, no tiredness: this my Dionysiac world which eternally creates itself, eternally destroys itself, this mystery-world of doubled desires, this my "Beyond Good and Evil", without goal, unless a goal lies in the pleasure of the circle, without will, unless a ring is full of will to turn on its own old course for ever around itself and only around itself: this my world—who is clear enough to look at it without wishing himself blindness? Strong enough, to hold his soul up to this mirror? His own mirror to the mirror of Dionysus? His own solution to the riddle of Dionysus? And he who should be able to do this, would he not then have to do still more? Betroth himself to the "Ring of Rings"? With the vow of his own recurrence? With the ring of eternal self-blessing, self-asseveration? With the will to will it all again and yet again? To will back all things which have ever been? To will forwards to everything which must ever be? Know ye now, what the world is for me? And what I desire, when I—desire this world?

CHAPTER VI

The Superman and the "Will to Power": Nietzsche's final ethical system

THOUGH there is a close connection between the "philosophy of the Superman" and the "philosophy of Dionysus", it is desirable to discuss them in separate chapters, for we have to approach them from different standpoints, and the main sources of evidence are not the same. The philosophy of the Superman includes the ideas of "Herrenmoral"—Master-morality—and "Will to Power". These ideas are also closely related to "the philosophy of Dionysus", but it would have been less suitable to treat them in that chapter.

Most people who have heard of Nietzsche, but have not read him, know that he talked about "Supermen". They probably know nothing else about him, unless they have heard of the phrase "blond beasts". There is no part of Nietzsche's philosophy which has been so widely disseminated as has the Superman idea, and none, except perhaps the cognate or dependent theories of "Immoralism" and the "Inversion of Ethical Values", which has been grossly misunderstood. Nothing else which Nietzsche said made such an easy appeal to half-educated minds; nothing lent itself so easily to the services of political or social propaganda; and nothing could be taken up so directly and so successfully by other writers. This is not the place in which to discuss the influence which Nietzsche has exerted, but I would remark in passing that the Superman seems to have gone bodily into Hofmannsthal, and Shaw, and others, that there has been, in the literature of the years since Nietzsche, a marked tendency to exalt *hardness*, and that it may even be reasonable to attribute four-fifths of the reaction which has taken place, in literature and in life, against the nineteenth century, to the influence of the Superman and the Supermorality.[1]

[1] The influence would be indirect, of course. Most of the people affected will never have read a line of Nietzsche. And I am not saying that the influence of the Superman part of Nietzsche's work

Dionysus, Recurrence, Superman; these ideas, and those dependent upon them, make up the most important part of Nietzsche's constructive philosophy, or, if one prefers it, of his religion, and in each of them there is a demonstrable resemblance to Greek thought, though it seems to me difficult or impossible to prove a definite *influence*. It is most difficult of all to prove that the Superman was taken from Greek literature or life: but most simple to point out what are the affinities.

In Nietzsche's first works there is nothing about any such ideas. *Die Geburt der Tragödie* is on quite different lines, and in *Unzeitgemässe Betrachtungen* Nietzsche defines the aim of evolution as "the coming into being of *true* men, and nothing else". In *Menschliches, Allzumenschliches* he speaks of "the perfect wise man", "the oligarchs of the spirit", and most frequently of "the good European". Spiritually Voltairean freethinkers, politically supernational, culturally cosmopolitan, the ideal men of Nietzsche's middle works are an easily recognisable, well defined type, represented in history by real characters. At this time Nietzsche considered that the Greeks conformed to the ideal. This is shown by a passage in *Morgenröte*: "The Greeks afford us the pattern of a race and culture which had grown pure: and it is to be hoped that some time a purely European race and culture will again be produced". In *Menschliches, Allzumenschliches* the use of the word "Übermensch"[1] is perhaps foreshadowed, in one place, by the description of man as "das Über-tier" (the super-animal), a phrase which may show that Nietzsche's thoughts were already beginning to run on these lines; and the theory of "Herrenmoral", the theory that there should be one system of morality for the strong, the rulers, and another for the weak, the slaves, is already evident in the same book, in aphorism 439. This passage also shows that Nietzsche believed that his own ideas on the comparative rights of the weak and the strong were the ideas of the ancient world.

---

is the most *valuable* part of his influence. I do not think that it is: but it is undoubtedly the most potent and most widespread.

[1] The term "Übermensch" is, of course, found at least as early as Goethe. See, for example, *Faust*, I, 490.

A higher culture can only come into existence, where there are two differentiated castes of society: that of the workers, and that of the leisured, those who are enabled to have real leisure: or, to use a stronger expression, the caste of forced labour and the caste of free labour...so speaks to us the fading voice of antiquity....

No doubt he was right, for slave-labour was indispensable to Greek and Roman civilisation. So, in aphorism 259, he emphasises that "the Greek culture of the classical period is a male culture". Women are like slaves—in fact they are slaves—and like slaves they are contemptible. Nietzsche's contempt for them is a Hellenic contempt.

So we see that even in *Menschliches*, *Allzumenschliches* Nietzsche is moving towards *Zarathustra*. There is one other point to notice in this. Throughout the book there is much insistence upon "ordering of society in classes", "higher and lower culture", and so on, though not with the violent emphasis of *Zarathustra* and the last works. It is typical of *Menschliches*, *Allzumenschliches* that the criticisms are mainly destructive, and also rather tentative. In the finished work, and in the fragments, there are two references to the phrase "Will to Power", but they are not of any especially great importance.

When we go on to *Morgenröte*, we find Nietzsche setting up an ideal of "a more than Greek social dignity". This is a form of "Herrenmoral", not yet so precise or so extreme as in the late works, but more emphatic than anything in *Menschliches*, *Allzumenschliches*. Let us look at aphorism 199:

"We are more distinguished." Loyalty, generosity of mind, the shame attached to one's good name: these three bound up together in one attitude of mind—that we call noble, distinguished, fine, and thereby we surpass the Greeks....In order to comprehend that the attitude of mind of the most distinguished Greeks, set beside our code of behaviour, which is still knightly and feudal, would inevitably be felt to be low and hardly decent, let us remember that word of consolation, which Odysseus has in his mouth when he is in a miserable situation: "Only bear it, my dear heart! Thou hast already borne things which were yet more fit for a dog!"...It was far from the minds of the Greeks to take life and death so lightly, on account of an insult, as we do...or to think more highly of preserving a good name than of acquiring a bad name, if the latter is compatible with glory and the feeling of power; or to keep faith with the prejudices and articles of belief of their own class, if those would prevent a man from becoming a tyrant. For this is the ignoble secret of each Greek aristocrat: from a feeling of the deepest jealousy he keeps every one of his own class on the same footing as himself, but is ready at every moment to fling himself like a tiger upon his prey, which is the overlordship: what does he care, in comparison, for lies, murder, treachery, betrayal of his own town? It was a matter of great difficulty for these men to practise justice...on seeing him who was most fortunate every man of high birth thought of the complete remorselessness and devilry of the tyrant, who sacrifices everything and everyone to his overweeningness and his desire....Men, whose lust for power no longer rages so blindly as did that of those high-born Greeks, no longer need that idolisation of the conception of the state, with which in those days that lust was kept in check.

Such "Machtgelüst" is not yet Nietzsche's own ideal, but later on it is. So when we read in Nietzsche's last works, *Zarathustra* and others, that this "Machtgelüst" is the noblest and most desirable quality of the human race, we must remember that he has already proved that he considered— rightly or wrongly—that precisely this "Machtgelüst" was the driving-power in Greek life. It is also implied in this passage that the ideal of "Vornehmlichkeit" has some connection with Greece, simply by the fact that Nietzsche speaks of the Greeks as examples of an ideal which it is necessary to sur- pass, as mediaeval manners had surpassed it. And it is true that Greek "nobility", καλοκἀγαθία, had none of the elaborate chivalry of mediaeval times: very likely because, as Nietzsche sees, Greek "Wille zur Macht" would not impose upon itself the fetters of an artificial code of honour and thereby impede or prevent the attainment of any important end.

In aphorism 38 of the same book, when speaking of the uncertainty of moral judgments—whence arises the argument for his own peculiar "Immoralism"—Nietzsche reminds us how different from men of to-day were "the older Greeks", particularly Hesiod, in their valuation of certain moral qualities. And when discussing the quality of pity, for which, now as always, he feels such deep distrust, he remarks that the Greeks felt, as he does, that pity is "a periodically re- curring unhealthy affliction, the dangerous nature of which can be done away with by momentary deliberate discharges". The chief danger is that pity, like an over-scrupulous code of honour, stands in the way of the "Will to Power".

As a matter of fact, Nietzsche's hatred for the quality of pity is as one-sided and as unfair as his hatred for Christianity, and for many others of his pet aversions. No doubt he had seen—how often, we wonder, in the cathedral town of Naumburg, in that hypocritical, pseudo-religious, pseudo-humane atmosphere of nineteenth-century Lutheran Saxony! and naturally, rightly, he had abominated—the particular manifestation of self-righteousness which masquerades as moral rectitude, and that curious but common ecclesiastical morbidity which appears in the cloak of compassion in order to lick its lips over the sight of the misfortunes of others. Let us look at *Morgenröte*, aphorism 224:

The "Elevating element in the misfortunes of one's neighbour". He is in misfortune, and now there come "the compassionate" and paint his misfortune for him in all its details—finally they go away satisfied and elevated: they have browsed on the horror of the unfortunate man as on their own horror, and have made themselves a pleasant afternoon.

Does anyone wonder that an honest man detested this all-too-frequent, all-too-human hypocrisy, and does anyone doubt that Nietzsche had seen much of this kind of thing, and little of any other kind of pity or humaneness? But does any reasonable man suppose that this is all there is in pity, or that Nietzsche had done more than see, and condemn, one highly objectionable perversion of a useful emotion? What he does once, here, he does many times, with many things, later on. This characteristic makes him more interesting but not more reliable.

Hardness is one of the most conspicuous qualities of the Superman, and in *Morgenröte*, aphorism 172, we find Nietzsche emphasising the hardness of the Greeks, in a way which few people, if any, would have been ready to do at that time. The passage "Tragödie und Musik" is particularly interesting and profound:

Men in a warlike fundamental state of mind, as for example the Greeks at the time of Aeschylus, are *hard to move*, and if for once pity conquers over their hardness, it takes hold of them like an intoxication and like a "demonic power"; they then feel themselves no longer free and moved by a religious horror. Afterwards they have their doubts about this state; as long as they are in it, they enjoy the ecstasy of being out of themselves and of the wonderful, mixed with the bitterest melancholy: that is so exactly a drink for warriors, something strange, dangerous, and bittersweet, which does not come to one easily. To souls which feel pity in this way, tragedy appeals, to hard and warlike souls, which are only conquered with difficulty, whether through fear or by pity, though it is useful to them from time to time to be *softened*.

Nietzsche realises so clearly—unlike his predecessors and contemporaries—that the Greeks were not a humanitarian race. He describes them in one passage as "barbarians of genius", and continually he stresses their hardness, their lack of sentimentality, their dependence upon slave-labour, and their contempt for women. "Hellenentum" is the perfect antithesis to Christianity, and in all these ways the Superman is the descendant of the Greeks.

Power, which has much evil done to it and thought against it, is worth more than impotence which only experiences good—so the Greeks felt. That is to say: the feeling of power was rated more highly by them than any advantage or good name.

So Nietzsche conceived the Greeks: not as conventional people then saw them, ideal, humane, contented denizens of a golden age, but as the ruthless, violent, unscrupulous personification of "Will to Power". Not yet did Nietzsche hold that *all* life and *all* activity are simply manifestations of this "Will to Power": in *Morgenröte*[1]—indeed, in all three books of his middle period—he is a determinist. It sounds curious, for Nietzsche, but it is none the less true. We *cannot will anything*; everything happens in accordance with preordained and immutable necessity. He abandons with great rapidity and with a fine disregard of consistency his determinism in favour of the theory that all the activities of life are unconstrained "Machtwille", but it is curious to find that in *Morgenröte* he speaks of Greek "Machtwille" side by side with unchangeable necessity.

[1] E.g. aphorism 124.

Die fröhliche Wissenschaft does not tell us much about "Will to Power", although R. M. Meyer sees, especially in the closing sections, some evidence that Nietzsche now entertained the aim of founding a new scientific *religion* based upon the *Will*. Life is to be regarded as an experiment in the pursuit of knowledge, with the multiplication of power as its practical end. It is true that we find passages bearing this meaning, but less stress is laid upon "Wille zur Macht" in *Die fröhliche Wissenschaft* than elsewhere. Not so with the Superman. *Die fröhliche Wissenschaft* is often curiously prophetic of *Zarathustra*, which follows it, and in a few sections the figure of Zarathustra the preacher actually appears.[1] While the good European or the "Freigeist" is still the ideal man, the term "Übermensch" is used for the first time. The passage, in which it is so used, deals with the advantages of polytheism, and the actual phrase is: "the invention of gods, heroes, and supermen of all kinds, as of creatures equal to men or below them...". We shall do well to notice that the Superman is first named alongside the Greek gods, although it would be rash to deduce that he is derived from the Olympians.

In all his works from *Menschliches, Allzumenschliches* onward Nietzsche stands in opposition to the commonly accepted standards, and even definitions, of Ethics. Ethical principles, he says, are the creation of the weak majority, and they are set up in order to repress the few strong characters. Such characters could not be prevented from attaining their ends at the expense of the weak, without the help which morality, especially Christian morality, affords to these. So all moral codes are fundamentally arbitrary; therefore they impose no obligation upon anyone who is strong enough to ignore them successfully. For the weak majority, ethical schemes are necessary, since nothing else can effectually protect them against the strong; and therefore the virtues of the mass of men may legitimately be valued by the measure of their compliance with their own "Herden-" or "Sklaven-moral". But this only applies to the mass: on the few who are strong and great these moral principles are not binding at all. The

[1] Section 342.

strong men can and must create their own "Herrenmoral". The limitations which they impose upon themselves will not be those of any Christian or conventional virtue, but simply such restrictions as will assist their "Will to Power".[1]

"I teach you the Superman", says Zarathustra: "God is dead: now let us will that the Superman live." Nothing that we have seen in the previous books, none of the hints that Nietzsche was groping his way towards a revolutionary ideal, has quite prepared us for the clear-cut uncompromising Superman-philosophy of *Zarathustra*. It is true that *Die fröhliche Wissenschaft* has already introduced us to that vigorous personality, and that the passages to which I have referred indicate how the main ideas of *Zarathustra* have gradually taken root in Nietzsche's mind—especially the ethical theory of "Herrenmoral" and "Sklavenmoral". Nevertheless, the sudden dawn of Nietzsche's third period is surprising or even startling, and there is every reason to believe him when, in *Ecce homo*, he describes it as a revelation.

Let us consider what the Superman really is, and let us also investigate his ancestry.

The term is not peculiar to Nietzsche. Many thinkers, before Nietzsche and since, have spoken about "Supermen": but Nietzsche's actual conception is, to put it mildly, unusual. The characteristics of his Superman and his super-civilisation are not such as other ethical speculators have generally thought desirable. As we might expect, Nietzsche is not consistent in his descriptions of the Superman, and these descriptions are not always clear. We are faced at the outset with a difficulty in determining whether the "Übermensch" is meant to be the sole inhabitant of a better future world—on this earth, of course—or a higher type to exist among ordinary men in the near future. Nietzsche sometimes says the one and sometimes the other: but though the inconsis-

[1] I am not at this moment concerned to criticise these opinions, but I should like to observe in passing that (1) Nietzsche's explanation of the origin of ethics is at any rate plausible, (2) his scheme for restoring the primitive uncontrolled rights of the strong man would lead to chaos. For a further discussion of this, see the next chapter.

tency is confusing, it is not of great importance, and it seems most probable that he usually conceives the "Übermensch" as something distant and difficult to produce. It also appears that in spite of his inconsistencies he hoped that the ideal future world would be inhabited by nothing but Supermen. It seems as if Nietzsche had reached his conception under the influence of the idea of evolution—which had gained more and more hold on him during the 'seventies—in combination with a Greek ideal. The gods of Greece, especially Apollo and Dionysus, and the half-gods, and the heroes, have been ever before his mind, and so, as he comes to believe more and more in the truth of the theory of evolution, he concludes that it is possible, and of course desirable, to develop men into something like the Greek gods or heroes. The "Aristocrats", and "oligarchs of the spirit", the "free spirits" and "good Europeans", Nietzsche's former ideal men, pale into insignificance as mere "higher men", who know that they are incomplete, and long to be perfected.[1] When the "Übermensch" comes, neither "higher" nor "last" men will exist any longer. They will either have been perfected, and become Supermen, or they will have died out.

The "Übermensch" is the personification of the *Will*, the "Will to Power", to complete self-development and self-expression.

Free callst thou thyself? Thy prevailing thought it is, that I wish to hear, and not that thou hast escaped from some yoke.

Art thou such a one as had a right to escape from a yoke? There is many a man who cast away his last value, when he cast away his state of service.

Free wherein? What cares Zarathustra for that? But thine eye shall proclaim to me clearly: free *to what end*?

That is the important point. The "Übermensch" shall be free for a positive end. He shall be a creator, like the Greeks; and all that hinders *creation* he must attack without mercy. The enemies of the creative force are the quiescent virtues, the mob, the state, most philosophies, and above all religion. "God is dead. Now let us will that the Superman live." And God is dead because he *pitied* men.

[1] Cf. *Also sprach Zarathustra*, book iv.

Dionysus is the god of dancing: Zarathustra is a dancer too. Dionysus loves laughter and revelry: so does Zarathustra.

I would only believe in a god (he says) who knew how to dance....So will I have man and woman: the one able to fight, the other able to bear children, *but both able to dance with head and legs*.

And let that day be accounted lost to us, on which there was not dancing once! And false be accounted to us every truth, along with which there was not laughter!

And thus speaks Zarathustra of the Will: "To redeem that which is past in man and to change the form of every 'it was' until the will speaks": "But so I desired it! So shall I desire it"...."All those are my equals, who give themselves their own will and cast away all submission from them." That is to say, a man must do what he wills, and must will what he does, unlike those detestable mediocrities "the good and just", who do what religion bids them, and have no will of their own. "Destroy for me, oh destroy for me", says Zarathustra, "the Good and Just."

Only the strong man will be truthful: the "good and just" never dare.

"Good men never speak the truth." But as the world is, the "good" men and the small men are the masters, with their kings and states and religions. "When shall I come again into my own country, where I do not have to bow myself any more—do not have to bow myself any more before the Small?" says the Superman, in words which he might have borrowed straight from Theognis or Pindar.

Freedom from ethical restrictions, for great ends; active, creative greatness; joy; these shall be good. Fetters shall be thrown off and authority denied. This life shall be accepted as the only life, and as good, though terrible. All that impedes greatness, power, beauty, shall be abolished. The fears of sin, hell, death, conscience, shall be exorcised. As there is no soul without body, there can be no spiritual greatness where the body is sick: therefore health is immeasurably valuable. Pity is a sickness or a selfishness. It hinders action, or serves to give an unhealthy pleasure to the pitier. Hardness is a virtue beyond all price.

"Why so hard?" said the kitchen coal once to the diamond: "Are we not then near relations?

"Why so soft? Oh my brothers, thus I ask you: are ye not then—my brothers?

"Why so soft, so yielding and submitting? Why is so much evasion, denial in your heart? So little fate in your gaze?

"And willed ye not to be fates and relentless: how could ye one day—conquer with me?

"And if your hardness will not flash, and cut, and cut in pieces: how could ye one day—create with me?

"For all creators are hard. And delight it must seem to you, to press your hand on centuries as on wax—

"Delight, to write on the will of centuries as on bronze—harder than bronze, nobler than bronze. Only the noblest is quite hard.

"This new commandment, oh my brothers, I put up over you: become hard!"

These are the qualities and the characteristics of the Superman: these are the new ideals: these are the things to which the efforts of men must be directed. All these qualities, characteristics, ideals, are summed up in the term "Wille zur Macht". Because Darwin believed that the driving-force of life was merely "Wille *zum Leben*", not "Wille zur Macht", Nietzsche abandoned Darwin and his own middle period of thought. The conception of life as "Wille zur Macht" forced him into his own independent, final Weltanschauung.

The books after *Zarathustra* are for the most part elaborations of one side or other of these ideas, and it is therefore only natural that our most accurate and detailed evidence should come from them. *Jenseits von Gut und Böse* and *Zur Genealogie der Moral* (the best of these last works) are really theses on the subject "Herrenmoral und Sklavenmoral". They keep fairly closely and logically to this aspect of the Superman-civilisation, not adding very much to what we have gleaned from earlier books, but amplifying and clarifying statements which have sometimes been obscure. There are consequently a number of passages in these works to which I should like to call attention. The first is the section of *Jenseits von Gut und Böse*, entitled "Was ist vornehm?" It runs as follows:

Every raising up of the type "man" was hitherto the work of an aristocratic society—and so it will always be: of a society, which believes in a long ladder of class-differentiation and of difference in value between man and man, and has need of slavery in some sense or other. Without the "Pathos of distance", as it grows up out of the deep-imprinted difference of the classes, out of the continual gaze outwards and downwards of the ruling caste upon subjects and instruments, and from their equally continual practice in obeying and commanding, in holding men down and at a distance, without this, I say, that other more mysterious pathos could not arise at all, that longing for an ever greater extension of distance within the soul itself...precisely the raising up of the type "man", the continual "self-conquest of man", to use a moral formula in a non-moral sense. Of course one must not abandon oneself to any humanitarian deceptions in regard to the history of the origin of an aristocratic society (that is, of the presupposition of any improvement of the type "man"): the truth is hard. Let us say to ourselves without sparing ourselves, how, up to now, every higher sort of culture on earth *began*! Men whose nature was still natural, barbarians in every fearful sense of the word, robber-men, still in possession of unbroken powers of will and lusts for power, hurled themselves upon weaker, more civilised, more peaceful races, or upon old decadent cultures, in which the last energy of life was just flickering out in dazzling fireworks of intellect and decay. The aristocratic caste was in the beginning always the barbarian caste: its preponderance of strength lay first of all not in physical strength, but in spiritual—those were the *more complete* men (a thing which, on every level, means in addition just about as much as "the more complete beasts").

"Härte und Heiterkeit" are the most desirable qualities for men. Those who are "hard and serene" will make a success of their lives, because they will naturally dominate and command. For a philosopher or psychologist it is absolutely necessary to have such a temper if he would avoid being overwhelmed by pity for his fellow-creatures.

But let Nietzsche speak again. His best definition of the origin and nature of "Herrenmoral" and "Sklavenmoral" is in the long aphorism 260 of *Jenseits von Gut und Böse*:

On a journey through the many finer and ruder types of moral codes, which have hitherto borne sway on earth, I found certain traits regularly recurring with each other and associated with each other: until finally two fundamental types betrayed themselves to me; and a fundamental difference sprang to light. There exist master-morality and slave-morality: I add at once that in all higher and more mixed cultures attempts at mediation between both types of morality come also into view, and still more often the simultaneous existence of both types and their mutual distrust, even occasionally their hard side by side existence—even in the same man, within one soul. The distinctions of moral values either came into existence under a ruling type of man, which grew conscious with a feeling of pleasure of its difference from the ruled type—or among the governed, the slaves and dependents of every degree. In the former case, when it is the rulers who settle the conception "good", then it is the elevated proud spiritual state, which is felt to be that which distinguishes and that which settles the ordering of classes. The noble man separates off from himself the beings in whom the opposite of such an elevated proud state finds expression: he despises them. Let us observe at once, that in this first sort of moral code the contrast "good" and "bad" (gut und *schlecht*) means as much as "noble" and "contemptible": the contrast "good" and "evil" (gut und *böse*) is of another origin. Despised is the coward, the timid man, the petty man, the man who thinks of his narrow profit: similarly the suspicious man, with his glance that is not free, the self-abaser, the doglike sort of man, who lets himself be mishandled, the begging flatterer, above all the liar: it is a fundamental belief of all aristocrats that the common people are untruthful.... The noble sort of man feels that he himself determines values: he does not need to let himself be approved, he judges thus: "what is harmful to me, that is harmful in itself"; he knows that it is he, who in the first place lends honour at all to things, he creates values. Everything which he knows in himself, he honours: such a kind of morality is self-glorification. In the foreground stand the feeling of fullness, of power which desires to overflow, the happiness of high tenseness, the consciousness of a richness, which would wish to give and to pay out: the noble man too helps the unfortunate, but never, or hardly ever, from pity, but more from an impulse, which is caused by the excess of power.... Noble and brave men, who think thus, are most widely removed from that type of morality which positively sees the token of morality in pitying, or in acting on behalf of others, or in désintéressement.... But a morality of the ruler is most foreign of all to present-day taste in the strictness of its principle that one only has duties towards one's equals! that towards the beings of lower rank, towards everything foreign, one may act according to one's own good will, or "as the heart wills", and in any case "beyond good and evil"; pitying and suchlike things may belong here. The capacity and duty to be grateful for a long time and to be revengeful for a long time—both only within the limits of one's equals—fineness in requital, a refinement of conception in friendship, a certain need to have enemies (so to speak as draining channels for the emotions of envy, combativeness, over-confidence—fundamentally, in order properly to be able to be a *friend*): all these things are typical tokens of the noble system of morality, which, as I have hinted, is not the morality of "modern ideas", and therefore is to-day hard to sympathise with, hard also to dig out and disinter. It is quite different with the second type of morality, with *Slave Morality*. It being assumed that the oppressed, subjected, suffering, those who are not free, those who are uncertain of themselves and tired, moralise—what will be the similar things in their moral scheme of values? Probably a pessimistic suspicion of the whole situation of man will find expression, perhaps a condemnation of man together with his situation. The gaze of the slave is unfavourable to the virtues of the mighty: he possesses scepticism and mistrust, he has fineness of mistrust against everything "good" which is honoured there—he would like to convince himself that happiness itself is not genuine there. On the contrary those qualities are brought forward and flooded with light, which serve to make easier the life of sufferers: here come pity, the kindly helping hand, the warm heart, patience, industry, humility, friendliness, into high honour, for those are here the useful qualities, and almost the only means whereby to endure the pressure of existence. Slave morality is essentially a morality of utility....[1]

Zur Genealogie der Moral proceeds still farther in enquiring into the nature of "Herrenmoral" and "Sklavenmoral". Nietzsche goes back to Greece, and discusses the etymology of καλὸς κἀγαθός and such terms. He finds that in all these terms—that is, terms which denote good and noble qualities— there are signs of the domination of one race over another, and of the prevalence of that true "Herrenmoral" which sees the small man, the man of the ruled classes, as inevitably bad, contemptible, and cowardly. All nations, all organisations of society, began with the conquest of the unfit, timid and peaceful, by the "blond beast sweeping magnificently after conquest and prey"—famous and ominous phrase: and because the "animals of prey" were able to conquer, they had a full right to do so, and a full right to use the conquered as they

---

[1] Let us notice the following three important points in *Jenseits von Gut und Böse*. The first two seem to be indications of Greek influence on Nietzsche's conception of "Herrenmoral". (1) In section 14 he speaks of "the Platonic way of thinking, which was an *aristocratic* way". (2) In section 49 he again describes Greek religion as "grateful and *aristocratic*". (3) In this book, for the first time, we find the whole cosmos explained as "Will to Power", the explanation being based upon a kind of scientific reasoning: "The world, seen from within, the world determined and characterised upon the basis of its 'intelligible character'—would be just 'Will to Power' and nothing more".

would. All early Greek civilisation was based upon this deep-rooted distinction between the brave and noble man who could do as he liked, and the cowardly common man who could not: and rightly so, for the qualities of the ἄριστοι, the natural and proper rulers, entitled them to absolute freedom and unchallenged supremacy.

The arrangement of human society in widely sundered classes is the work of the human will. In that arrangement the will is operating in accordance with the laws of nature, and therefore the class-system, as it is found in primitive societies, is good. But the will does not always operate "according to nature", for Religion, God, Devil, Hell, and all our choicest spiritual torments, are also the work of the will and of nothing else.

That will to self-torment...a sort of will-madness in spiritual cruelty, which simply has no equal: the *will* of man to find himself guilty and reprehensible to the point of being irredeemable, his *will* to imagine himself punished, without the possibility that the punishment can ever become equivalent to the guilt, his *will* to infect and make poisonous the deepest foundation of things with the problem of guilt and punishment, in order once for all to cut off for himself the exit from this labyrinth of "fixed ideas", his *will* to set up an ideal—that of his "sacred God"—in order, in face of this, to become palpably certain of his absolute unworthiness....

And, as in religion, so in every social and political form lies hidden the "Will to Power", the "Will to Rule", as in Greece:

Beneath every oligarchy lies hidden always—the whole of history teaches it—the lust of tyranny; every oligarchy is continually trembling as a result of the tension, which every single individual in it must undergo, in order to remain master over this lust. (So it was for example in *Greece*: Plato testifies to it in a hundred passages, Plato, who knew his equals—*and* himself....)

In the epilogue to *Der Fall Wagner* there is one most important contribution to the study of "Herrenmoral". This is a passage which contrasts these principles of morality with the Christian principles, much in the same way as Dionysus is contrasted with Christ in *Ecce homo*. The passage is almost as significant as *Ecce homo* in showing the close connection between "Herrenmoral" and Dionysus.

In the narrower sphere of so-called moral values no greater contrast can be found than that of a master-morality and of the morality of the *Christian* conceptions of value: the latter grown upon a thoroughly morbid soil...master-morality, on the other hand (Roman, heathen, classical, Renaissance) as the sign-language of healthfulness, of *ascending* life, of the will to power as principle of life. Master-morality *affirms* just as instinctively as Christian morality *denies* (God, the Other World, self-abnegation, all mere negations). The former contributes from its own fullness to other things—it transfigures, it makes beautiful, it *makes the world reasonable*—the latter makes the value of things poorer, paler, uglier, it *denies* the world.

So too: "aristocratic morality, master-morality—the essence of both is gratitude". This is another declaration of the Dionysiac outlook on life, "the highest formula of asseveration", the acceptance of *all* that life brings. "Master-morality" is a means and a standard to attain that end.

In *Götzendämmerung* we find the most interesting passages on this subject in "Was ich den Alten verdanke". Let us first notice what Nietzsche says about "Herrenmoral" in Greece, and about the qualities of the Superman. Realism, hardness, inhumaneness, are the characteristic qualities of the Greeks: this is best shown by Thucydides.

My cure, my preference, my course of healing from everything Platonist was at all times *Thucydides*. Thucydides and perhaps the Prince of Machiavelli are most closely related to myself through the unconditional will to pretend nothing, and to see reason in reality, not in the "reason", far less in "morality"....Nothing cures one so thoroughly from the miserable beautification of the Greeks into an ideal, as Thucydides....In him the *Sophist-culture*, I mean the *Realist-culture*, finds its completed expression: this priceless movement in the midst of the moral-swindle of the Socratic schools which was just then breaking loose everywhere. Greek philosophy as the decadence of the Greek instinct; Thucydides as the great sum, the last revelation of that strong, strict, hard, matter-of-factness, which was instinctive in the older Hellenes....

Even more definite, clear, and important is the next paragraph:[1]

[1] These passages are the most direct and challenging contradiction of the Goethe-Schiller-Winckelmann conception of Greece that Nietzsche ever wrote. At that time (1887) they must have sounded almost blasphemous; to-day they are excellent, but *rather obvious*, good sense.

To discover in the Greeks "beautiful souls", "golden means", and other perfections, to admire, perhaps, in them a repose in greatness, an ideal frame of mind, a high simplicity—from this "high simplicity", essentially a niaiserie allemande, I was protected by the psychologist whom I bore within me. I saw their strongest instinct, the "Will to Power", I saw them tremble before the uncontrolled force of this instinct, I saw all their institutions grow out of measures taken for safety, in order to make themselves secure against their inner explosive material. The tremendous tension within then unloaded itself in fearful and remorseless hostility without: the town communities tore each other to pieces, in order that the citizens of each individual one might find security against themselves. It was found necessary to be strong: danger was near, it lurked everywhere....

Nietzsche nowhere states so explicitly as this that he conceived the Greeks to have been the supreme examples of his own "Wille zur Macht". It does not follow that he acquired his own idea *from observation of the Greeks*: but when we remember his early studies, not forgetting that his favourite figures in Greek literature were the Sophists, the early philosophers, the early lyric poets, the tyrants, Thucydides, have we not reasonable justification for thinking that he may have learned from them?

Der Antichrist begins with some further definitions of "Will to Power" and the associated ideas, in a form which now seems to be growing exaggerated.

What is good? Everything which increases the feeling of power, the will to power, power itself in man.

What is bad? Everything which emanates from weakness.

What is happiness? The feeling that power *grows*—that a resistance is being overcome.

Not satisfaction, but more power; *not* peace at all, but war; *not* virtue, but efficiency (virtue in the Renaissance style, virtu, virtue which is free from morality-poisoning).

The weak and misbegotten must perish: first statement of *our* love of mankind. And one must actually help them thereto.

What is more harmful than any vice? Pity, in practice, for all that is misbegotten and weak—Christianity....

The book goes on to explain the need of willing, breeding, and developing a higher type of man; but not the Superman of *Zarathustra*. The ideal man is again, as in Nietzsche's second period, the "higher man", a type which, in *Zarathustra*, he condemned.

The problem is, what type of man one shall *breed*, shall *desire*, as possessing higher value, more worthy of life, more certain of a future.

This type of higher value has already existed quite often: but as a stroke of fortune, as an exception, never as *desired*. On the contrary it is just he that has been most feared; he was up to now almost *the* fearful thing. . . .

This type of being has existed in the world, above all at times such as the Renaissance, and he occasionally even appears at the present day—or might so appear. But the ordinary (unplanned) development of the human race will not necessarily lead to any sort of real improvement in the human type, and indeed it almost certainly will not bring about any such result if it is left to its own unaided efforts. On the other hand (says Nietzsche) it does happen that every now and again, in the most diverse circumstances and places, these individuals of a higher type appear by accident, and they appear "in comparison with the whole of the human race, as a sort of Superman". Indeed it may even happen that whole races or peoples will appear as such successful higher types.

This, after *Zarathustra*, is an extremely curious reversion to earlier ideas ("guter Europäer", "vollkommener Weiser", and so on). Although the term "Übermensch" is here used, it conveys an entirely different meaning. There is no doubt that Zarathustra's Superman is a being who has never yet trodden the earth, something far above the most splendid examples of humanity in history. "As man is to the ape, so shall the Superman be to man." But the Superman of *Der Antichrist* has existed in the past, and may even exist to-day. What are we to understand by this glaring inconsistency? Is it merely one of our author's arbitrary, perhaps deliberate, caprices? Or are we to suppose that Nietzsche did not intend *Zarathustra* to be taken quite literally? That it really contains much which is exaggeration or poetical genius, not practical advice? Or after all, is it simply that *Der Antichrist* is intended to be more practical, to set a more limited and more easily attainable limit to our vision, to show us how to bring about not "Socialism" but "Immoralism" in our time?

In paragraph no. 7 of *Der Antichrist* we find another excellent statement of Nietzsche's reasons for hating pity. In the first place, pity makes a man depressed and lethargic, and so counteracts his "Will to Power" and his energies: this argument we have had before. In the second place (this, Nietzsche now says, is more important), pity tends to prevent the survival of the fittest, because it preserves that which, being weak, ought to perish.

In general pity crosses the law of development, which is the law of *selection*. It preserves that which is ripe for dissolution, it maintains itself in favour of the disinherited and condemned of life, and through the amount of misbegottenness of every sort, which it preserves alive, it gives life itself a gloomy and questionable aspect. People have dared to call pity a virtue (in every *aristocratic* system of morality it counts as a weakness); indeed they have gone further, they have made it into *the* virtue, the origin and foundation of all virtues.... Schopenhauer was right about it: through pity life is denied, made *more worthy of denial*—pity is the practice of Nihilism....[1]

This is the principal evidence concerning Superman, Supermorality, and "Will to Power", up to *Der Wille zur Macht*. As usual, this last book does not add anything new. It explains, co-ordinates, arranges; multiplies arguments and examples; creates a system. Nevertheless, the very title of the work indicates how Nietzsche has become more and more

---

[1] Nietzsche has suffered much from being interpreted by unbalanced persons, who have read into passages like this meanings which have obscured the perfectly sound sense underlying the rather noisy sentences: for it is not a good thing, but a very bad thing, to shelter, preserve, and cause to multiply, unsound stocks like the feeble-minded, the inebriate, the consumptive, and the syphilitic. But the real reason why such undesirable and detrimental types continue and increase is that sentimental, compassionate, and above all religious prejudices prevent their extirpation by sterilisation and other means. Yet all sensible and clear-sighted men, even the most humane and sympathetic, would agree that drastic action against such perils is urgently necessary, and that, if we eliminate the exaggerations of language which are natural to one of his temperament, Nietzsche is perfectly right.

obsessed by the conception of the universe
Power". In the arrangement of the fragments
Brahn, the editor of the volume (no. IX) in th
Ausgabe, even the headings of the different sectio
sweeping, yet how reasoned, is this belief that all
to Power". We thus find: "The intellect—a wil
nature—a will to power; society—a will to power; art—a will
to power". But Nietzsche is not *only* concerned to demon-
strate that all our activities are "Will to Power". He insists,
as before, that we must free ourselves from Christian or
conventional ethics. He demands, as before, that the man
who has the strength and the purpose to be above morality,
shall be above it. He urges, as before, that we must allow a
different set of virtues to slaves and rulers.

Modest, industrious, full of good will, moderate: so you desire
man? the *good man*? But it seems to me that that is only the ideal
slave, the slave of the future.

Homo natura. The will to power! The moral values as *values of
outward appearance*, compared with the *physiological values*.

All movements, all types of men, have been sustained
through the ages by the "Will to Power", and by nothing
else. All social, religious, political, ethical systems are merely
the expression of the "Will to Power" in one form or another.
Where the will could be assisted by an arbitrarily constructed
system of ethics—and the will of the weak and small has
always desired such systems—then ethics have sprung into
being. And as a rule, in past history, the will of the weak and
small has lamentably succeeded in asserting itself. Nevertheless these weak creatures, the numerical majority, have no
right to force through their own "Will to Power", and impose
their ethical systems upon the world. This right belongs only
to the strong, to those who are above all moral or religious
scruples. Therefore—Rangordnung; "Herrenmoral" for the
strong, "Sklavenmoral" for the weak.

I am driven, in the age of universal suffrage, that is to say, when
everyone is allowed to sit in judgment over everyone and everything,
to restore *the ordering of men in ranks*.

I teach that there exist higher and lower men, and that in certain
circumstances an individual can justify the existence of whole

centuries.... The rank of men is settled and altered by their degree of power alone, and by nothing else.... He who settles values and guides the will of thousands of years by guiding the highest men, is *the highest man*.... In spite of all the efforts of three thousand years we have not yet reached again the level of the *Renaissance man*, and in his turn the Renaissance man remained behind *the man of antiquity*.

This rapid examination of the Superman, his code of ethics, and his "Will to Power", should leave us in no doubt of what Nietzsche meant by these ideas or of how he explains them. We should not expect him to provide us with anything in the nature of a formal proof; for it is clear that Nietzsche's beliefs and ideals are based entirely upon quasi-religious conviction, buttressed up by historical example. Nietzsche traces the evolution of ethics from the past, not by careful reasoning, but by dogmatic statements which sometimes seem to be inspired by an instinctive, but inexplicable, sense for what is true. From his survey of past history he deduces the general principle, true of all times and all circumstances, that life is "Wille zur Macht". From this "law of nature", again, he deduces his ideal for the future development of civilisation. Whether he is right or wrong, this is his line of thought, in so far as we can speak of a line of thought; for often he progresses in a series of leaps, sometimes successful, sometimes disastrous, but always hazardous. Nor must we forget that Nietzsche often starts by leaping, and then makes up an argument to justify himself for having leapt.

We could spend much time and space and trouble in criticising Nietzsche's ethics as herein expounded, and we should no doubt decide that, however he reached his conclusions, logically or illogically, they are, like most things, a blend of truth and falsehood, sense and nonsense. But I do not propose to attempt to criticise them here.[1] I want to consider one further problem only in connection with these ideas, namely the problem of their derivation from Greek thought. It is certain that this is not their only source, for Nietzsche was undoubtedly influenced, in his Superman theories,

[1] See pp. 150–156, where I have embarked upon a not very extensive criticism.

by philosophers other than Greek, for example by Stirner and Kierkegaard.[1] But partly? Is there not a substantial connection between the Superman, "Herrenmoral", "Will to Power", and Greece?

The connection is probably even more substantial than has yet been recognised. Of course, Nietzsche virtually says so again and again; as in the last sentence which I quoted above. "We have not yet reached again the level of the *Renaissance man*, and in his turn the Renaissance man remained behind *the man of antiquity*." Now if the "antike Menschen" excelled the men of the Renaissance, they must have been well on the way to the Superman, for Nietzsche continually says that the Renaissance was a period in which a high type of man, an "all-but-Superman", flourished. Some Renaissance characters—for example Cesare Borgia, "eine Art Übermensch", and Machiavelli—are actual embodiments of his ideal, as are a few other historical personages, such as Napoleon. But the Greeks were still nearer to the ideal. I have just quoted a passage from *Götzendämmerung*,[2] which shows that he considered "Wille zur Macht" to have been the dominant impulse in all Greek life; and I could quote many more, for whenever Nietzsche discusses Will and Ethics he reveals, explicitly or implicitly, that he believed the Greeks thought as he did.

But did they? It would be possible, or rather easy, for Nietzsche to misconceive the Greek Weltanschauung and the Greek character, especially when (1) he is passionately attached to his own conceptions, (2) he passionately admires the Greeks, (3) he would therefore gladly believe that they thought like himself, and that he was their spiritual descendant. But actually I think that he did not misconceive the nature of the Greeks. As usual, he portrays them in colours which must have seemed, did seem, utterly repugnant to his contemporaries, for he sees them in an entirely new light: but this fact simply shows that, once again, he has more insight, surer

[1] There is also the Faust-tradition, which must have played a considerable rôle in shaping Nietzsche's conception.

[2] See above, pp. 133–134.

instincts, more "psychologisches Feingefühl", than anyone else of his time. Let us briefly consider whether the Greeks were at all like the Superman, whether their "working code of ethics" was anything like Nietzsche's, and whether Greek life was all undisguised "Will to Power".

I do not think that any Greek poet or philosopher said, like Nietzsche: "Life and the universe are simply 'Will to Power'". Indeed I do not think that anyone except Nietzsche has ever said so. Will to Life, Struggle for Existence, Survival of the Fittest, Natural Selection, and similar definitions of life, are found in various thinkers, including Greek thinkers: but all these conceptions are widely different from Nietzsche's. But though no Greek philosopher ever used the term "Will to Power", or defined life's manifestations in Nietzsche's way, is there not a much wider truth in what he says? Is he not right when he claims that Greek life was "Will to Power"? Indeed, did not the most clear-sighted Greek thinkers and writers recognise this fact? In the passage from *Was ich den Alten verdanke*, already cited,[1] Nietzsche comments carefully and accurately upon the Greek "Will to Power". What were its consequences? In politics it led to the existence of small communities, which waged frightful wars among each other, principally in the age of Pericles and later. Formerly there had been violent internal struggles in almost every single state: Tyranny, Oligarchy, Democracy, political feuds and hatreds; restless colonisation, the banishment of political factions, trade rivalry and trade wars, like the Trojan war. In art we see an extraordinary brilliance, also brought about by "Wille zur Macht"; the competitions in Tragedy, the reckless beautification of Athens in her days of supremacy. We see the athletic contests, the Olympic and other games, the honour given to the victors, and the intense desire for physical distinction. We see the inability of the Greeks to combine for long, even for the most obvious common good, their inability to maintain a political alliance, so that Greek civilisation and independence were always insecure, and soon collapsed. Surely the whole history of the Greek states is

[1] P. 133 f.

the story of the struggle for supremacy, on the part of single states and individual persons, which prevented strength, permanence, or security, and destroyed that from which it arose? Against the Persians most of the Greeks combined, though even in face of this danger jealousy or internecine hatreds caused some to abstain: but as soon as the invasion had been defeated, the combination fell completely to pieces, and we see the Greek commander-in-chief[1] taking bribes from his enemy, the principal states intriguing against one another, and soon on the brink of civil war. All that is said in praise of Greek political genius seems to me to be outweighed by their inability ever to bury their mutual jealousies and to form any larger society than their city states. Their statesmen, except for a few like Epaminondas of Thebes, could see nothing but what was immediately in front of their noses; and all the greatness of a Pericles in managing Athens' internal affairs does not atone for his embarking on a Peloponnesian war. Athens reached her little summit of power, and could not rest there. She must needs seek more, and so she brought her world down in ruins upon her head. We have already noted Nietzsche's great admiration for Thucydides. Thucydides shows us, with his own unique, clear, relentless objectivity, just what the Greeks of his time were. Nietzsche admires Thucydides because he shows us the Greeks as they were; and he admires the Greeks for being as Thucydides shows them, all unrestrained, unashamed "Machtwille".

And the picture shows every sign of being true. No enraptured veneration of a golden Hellenic civilisation ought to survive one reading of Thucydides. Let us call to mind the case of the Melians,[2] helpless and inoffensive neutrals in the

[1] Pausanias.

[2] There are two references in Nietzsche to the Melian Dialogue which show that he was fully alive to its significance, and that he judged it to be typical of the Greeks. The first is from *Menschliches, Allzumenschliches*, aphorism 92: "Origin of justice. Justice (fairness) originates as between men who are more or less *equally powerful*, as Thucydides (in the fearful conversation between the Athenian and Melian envoys) rightly conceived it: when there exists no clearly recognisable superiority of power, and a struggle

great Peloponnesian war, upon whom the Athenians desired, for no good reason, to enforce a humiliating submission. The Melians refused to submit, claiming with justice that they were harmless and well-disposed people, whereupon the Athenians, expressly denying that weak states or weak individuals have any rights,[1] captured and destroyed the town of Melos and its population.

The Melian Dialogue is the most famous passage in Thucydides in which we are shown the inhumanity and hardness of the Athenians; but it is by no means the only one. The historian's tone is in fact everywhere the same.[2] Everywhere he calmly and impartially describes a people which was dominated by an irresistible and relentless passion to rule. He never condemns this passion, and there is no reason to suppose that he felt it deserved condemnation.

But, as the Melian Dialogue has shown us, the Greek character is governed, not merely by "Will to Power", but by *unscrupulous* "Will to Power". The Melian Dialogue illustrates

would result in fruitless and mutual damage, then there arises the thought of coming to an understanding and negotiating about the claims of both sides: the original character of justice lies in the character of exchange...". The main importance of this passage, in which the Melian Dialogue is still a fearful thing, not a splendid example of "Machtwille", is to show how Nietzsche regards it as illustrating something very fundamental about moral positions, namely their relative character. The second passage is from *Der Wille zur Macht*: "Does anyone perhaps think that the little Greek free cities, which would gladly have eaten each other up with fury and envy, were guided by humane and upright principles? Does anyone perhaps make a reproach to Thucydides out of the speech, which he put into the mouth of the Athenian envoys, when they negotiate with the Melians about destruction or submission?..." Here Nietzsche is arguing in favour of the attitude of open contempt to all professions of principle, as exemplified by the Sophists, and there can be no doubt that his attitude not only to the dispassionate narrative of Thucydides, but even to the action of the Athenians against Melos, was one of approval. Because the Athenians had the true "Wille zur Macht", they were justified in acting as they desired.

[1] "Right, as the world goes, is only in question between equals in power, while the strong do what they can, and the weak suffer what they must."

[2] Contrast the passionate moral indignation of the *Roman* Tacitus.

this fact in the harshest lights, but there are other instances just as harsh; and I have no doubt that the Superman's hardness, and his indifference to suffering, pain, and injustice are coloured by the hardness and indifference which appear from time to time as fundamental qualities of the Greeks. Nietzsche's dislike of pity is shared by nearly all the Greeks. Not by Plato, whom Nietzsche calls a decadent: but by the more genuinely *Greek* people.   For example, most of the heroes of Greek tragedy, in their determination to attain their ends, show an inhumaneness which to us is far from admirable. To be deterred by any feelings of pity would have seemed to them extremely foolish. The Greek gods do not pity the sufferings of mankind. They are interested or entertained spectators, in all Greek poetry from Homer onwards. The typical Greek hero is Odysseus. There is no question that his character was widely admired by the Greeks, and no doubt either that whether it is drawn by Homer in the *Odyssey*, by Sophocles in the *Philoctetes*, or by any other poet, its salient feature is always unscrupulousness. He conforms precisely to Nietzsche's ultimate conception of "moralinfreie Tugend", the "virtu" of the Renaissance, by which the power and will to an end confer the right to use all methods to reach it. Equally Nietzschean is Odysseus' complete indifference, in Sophocles' play, to the fate of Philoctetes, provided his own design can be accomplished.

So it is with Kreon in the *Oedipus Tyrannus*. Kreon is only a secondary character, not a hero who brings a tragic fate upon himself, nor a villain held up to reprobation. On the contrary, he is an ordinary "good" man, who rescues from the ruin of Oedipus' life as much as can be saved, and stands amid the horror and pain of the final scenes as the representative of that which is right and fitting.[1] But because he is the "proper man", the good man, the gentleman, he acts, as we should say, hardly and almost cruelly to Oedipus. For he abruptly cuts short his lamentations, and makes him leave the scene of his vanished glories, to go forth as an exile and a

[1] I do not think there is any doubt that the dramatist and the Greek spectator saw Kreon in this light.

wanderer, not because he had intentionally committed a sin, but because Heaven's anger was on him, therefore it would be dangerous to treat him kindly. It *would not do*. This single instance, in a character of secondary importance (and therefore all the more likely to be realistically drawn), illustrates the point extremely well. The Greek ideal was quite unlike the theoretical (but unrealised) ideal of the modern world, which is partly based upon Christianity, and partly upon the ethical teaching of those who, like Kant, see virtue in self-abnegation. The great Greek ideal was an ideal of physical beauty, power, and success, ability to attain one's own ends, provided those ends satisfied one's own judgment. Typical of it are Demosthenes, Odysseus, imperial Athens, Themistocles, or the heroes of the Pindaric hymns. Pindar is sometimes very near to Nietzsche, nowhere nearer than when he exalts the prowess and beauty of triumphant victors. It is an aspect of Greek life which has not been readily or willingly recognised by Greek scholars of the traditional conservative school, but Nietzsche, who saw much farther than most scholars, even if he did not always see straight, understood how little the Greeks had in common with any Christian or modern European ideal, and how untrue it was to call them humane at heart. So, when he tells us that his ideal man is one who is anything rather than humane, sympathetic, or unselfish, he is virtually telling us that his ideal man is like a Greek. Nor, when we consider how much time Nietzsche had spent on Hellenic studies, can we call the similarity a coincidence. We should find, if we pursued our investigation into the Greek character, that what I have just said holds good of almost all the characters of all Greek writers, of Homer, Pindar, Sophocles, and—most significantly—of Euripides. For Euripides takes the glorious, famous, admired hero, overdraws him a little, and makes him—repulsive. Nor are the Greek gods the deities of a humane race. We have only to consider for a moment the traditional character of Zeus, Apollo, or Hermes, as portrayed in the myths; while historical figures such as Themistocles or Alcibiades are as unscrupulous, as hard, and as vulgar, as Zeus himself.

So much for the Superman and his Greek ancestry. If we now turn to Nietzsche's theory of Ethics, we shall find something very like his "Immoralism" in the Greek philosophers. In Nietzsche's "kinsman" Heraclitus we find the idea that the universe is a game played by Zeus. This is a denial of the existence or validity of any moral scruple or moral principle; and both this same conception and the closest parallels to it— for example the statement that the world exists merely to provide a *spectacle* for the gods—are found several times in Nietzsche. Moreover, the conception of "Herrenmoral" and "Sklavenmoral", if it is not actually implicit in all Greek thought down to Socrates, is certainly explicitly stated by Theognis, in whom Nietzsche was always especially interested.

In the relationship of Nietzsche to Theognis we have probably got the most tangible evidence of Greek influence on our philosopher's ethics. The connection began early in Nietzsche's life, but this fact does not militate against the probability of a lasting influence. We know that other permanent influences originated in Nietzsche's university or school days,[1] so that there is no reason to argue that his early interest in Theognis' works should have died out and left no trace.

We remind ourselves that Nietzsche made a special study of Theognis for the purpose of writing two essays or treatises, one at Schulpforta, the other, a learned and valuable revision and expansion of it, at Leipzig University. Though in themselves these essays are not of any extraordinary merit, but just good of their kind, it really seems to have been his study of Theognis, for the purpose of writing them, which first drew Nietzsche's attention to the possibility of variable or arbitrary ethical standards. He found, apparently to his astonishment, that Theognis, the aristocratic poet who despised the mob, called those things good, which distinguished the nobly born man, and those bad, which did not, paying no attention to any other ethical standards or criteria of his own time; and flatly contradicting the fundamental beliefs of the present day. How near he was, in doing this,

---

[1] For example that of Hölderlin, which goes back at least to 1867.

to the Nietzschean ideas of "Herrenmoral" and "Sklaven-moral" we need hardly emphasise at this point. *Zur Genea-logie der Moral*, in particular, might have been written by a philosophising, rather prosaic Theognis.

Pindar, like Theognis, makes moral excellence synonymous with excellence of birth and athletic prowess. No one who is not one of the "Herren", no one who does not possess these qualities, is worth his consideration. The ugly, weak, low-born man is a creature of an inferior order, with none of the same rights. And let us remember once more that Greek and Roman civilisation was based upon slavery, the absolute negation of any belief that men are equal or that all men have rights, a conception which Nietzsche more than once went out of his way to applaud. His future civilisation, with its "Herrenmoral" and "Sklavenmoral", is just as truly founded upon slavery as was the ancient world.

Next let us cast a glance upon the Sophists.

The Sophist-culture (says Nietzsche), I mean the realist-culture...this priceless movement in the midst of the moral- and ideal-swindle of the Socratic schools which was everywhere breaking out just at that time.

The *Sophists* are nothing more than realists...they have the courage, which all strong spirits have, to *know* about their amorality.

The Sophists were Greeks: when Socrates and Plato took the side of virtue and justice, they were Jews or I do not know what. The tactics of Grote in order to defend the Sophists are wrong: he desires to elevate them into men of honour and moral standards—but their honour was, not to carry on any swindle with big words and virtues....

Even more significant as an illustration of Nietzsche's position in regard to Thucydides and to the Sophists, and of the close connection which he supposed to exist between them, is *Morgenröte*, aphorism 168:

What do I love in Thucydides, how does it come about that I honour him more highly than Plato? He has the widest and most natural joy in everything typical in men and events, and finds that to every type there *belongs a quantum of good sense: this* he seeks to discover. He has a greater degree of practical justice than Plato: he is no slanderer and disparager of the men whom he does not like, or who have hurt him in life....So comes in him, the thinker about men, that *culture of the most natural knowledge of the world* to a last magnificent flowering period, a culture which had its poet in Sophocles, its statesman in Pericles, its doctor in Hippocrates, its natural scientist in Democritus: that culture which deserves to be baptised in the name of its teachers the *Sophists*, and unfortunately begins from this moment of baptism suddenly to become pale and incomprehensible to us, for we now suspect that it must have been a very unmoral culture, against which a Plato fought, together with all the Socratic schools....

With Nietzsche's criticisms that ethical rules are the creation of the weak against the strong, a series of arbitrary regulations generally supported by untrue claims to revelation, with his argument that morality is a variable, relative thing, we must compare several points in the teachings of the Sophists.

Protagoras and his famous saying: πάντων μέτρον ἄνθρωπος (man is the measure of all things), that is, there is no such thing as an absolute ethical standard—Nietzsche considered to be very modern and very like himself. "Our way of thought to-day is in a high degree Protagorean." We should not go far astray if we took Protagoras' sentence as the foundation of Nietzsche's philosophy, as his basic condition of all truth. Upon nothing does he insist more continually than that one cannot set up anything as absolute truth, that the judgment of men—and not even the best men—has been responsible for all ethical ideas and systems; in a word, that "man is the measure of all things".

There are several other points of contact. We find, for instance—this also in Protagoras—that the *State* determines what shall be considered good and bad. Hippias says that human law and nature should be completely dissociated; Thrasymachus, that justice emanates from the strong, and that injustice is something stronger, nobler, and more mighty than justice; Callicles, that moral ideas were invented by the weak majority in order to suppress the strong minority.

By the rule of nature, to suffer injustice is the greater disgrace because the greater evil; but conventionally, to do evil is the more disgraceful. For the suffering of injustice is not the part of a man but of a slave, who indeed had better die than live; since when he is wronged and trampled upon, he is unable to help himself, or any other about whom he cares. The reason, as I conceive, is that the makers of laws are the majority who are weak; and they make laws and distribute praises and censures with a view to themselves and their own interests; and they terrify the stronger sort of men, and those who are able to get the better of them, and they say, that dishonesty is shameful and unjust; meaning, by the word injustice, the desire of a man to have more than his neighbours....And therefore the endeavour to have more than the many is conventionally said to be shameful and unjust, and is called injustice, whereas Nature herself intimates that it is just for the better to have more than the worse, the more powerful than the weaker; and in many ways she shows, among men as well as among animals, and indeed among whole cities and races, that justice consists in the superior ruling over and having more than the inferior....Nay, but these are the men who act according to nature; yes, by Heaven, and according to the law of nature: not, perhaps, according to that artificial law, which we invent and impose upon our fellows, of whom we take the best and strongest from their youth upwards, and tame them like young lions—charming them with the sound of the voice, and saying to them, that with equality they must be content, and that the equal is the honourable and the just. But if there were a man who had sufficient force, he would shake off and break through, and escape from all this; he would trample under foot all our formulas and spells and charms, and all our laws which are against nature: the slave would rise in rebellion and be lord over us, and the light of natural justice would shine forth.

This speech comes from the *Gorgias* of Plato;[1] and in more than one other passage from the same work we observe a Nietzschean enthusiasm for that form of heroic greatness which would disdain all conventional moral restraints, and impose its own will upon ordinary people.

Of course, the conditions are not the same. The arguments of the Sophists were often mere dialectical exercises which were not meant sincerely, whereas Nietzsche, except when he just sets out to shock or startle people, is absolutely in earnest. It would be a mistake to insist upon too close a connection or too great an influence. But it is indisputable that both the Sophists and Nietzsche repeatedly put a question mark against moral positions, though Nietzsche did so with an entirely moral purpose: "I had to do away with morality in order to make my moral will prevail".

[1] The sentiments expressed in it are (of course) subsequently refuted by Socrates.

We conclude by returning to something which we have said before, namely this. It is not so much that connections exist between Nietzsche and this or that definite Greek writer or work. We can bring up these and other instances of a very close resemblance on certain points; and we can justifiably argue from them that there is an influence of the one upon the other. But *essentially* we are concerned, as Nietzsche was, with a wider conception of Greece. We find that Nietzsche thought that the Greeks were the same kind of people as he meant his Superman to be, inspired by the same "Will to Power" and the same Dionysiac enthusiasm, and generally in agreement with his own belief in the limited validity of any ethical code. This view of Greece is widely accepted to-day as a true picture, whereas when Nietzsche first put it forward he was universally derided. But the more carefully and impartially we consider the history, institutions, habits, religion, and literature of Greece, the more we shall be led to agree that he was right.

CHAPTER VII

Some criticisms of Nietzsche's Weltanschauung, and of his "optimism"

T HOSE whose opinions are most to be respected have nearly always maintained that Nietzsche was an optimist who tried to inspire others to adopt a hopeful and profitable view of life. "This optimistic and individualistic reaction" (against Hegel and Schopenhauer), says Professor J. G. Robertson, "is most clearly set forth in the work of Friedrich Nietzsche, the most original thinker in the last period of German intellectual evolution.... Wagner and Nietzsche held irreconcilable Weltanschauungen—Wagner, that pessimism which, for the greater part of a century, had dominated German culture, Nietzsche, a new, individualistic, joyous optimism." "Nietzsche", says Oskar Walzel, "refutes Schopenhauer's pessimism and sets forth optimistically...to set the will free. The one seeks morality in the denial, the other in the affirmation of the being of the world. The one demands weakness of will, the other strength of will."

It is from these judgments that we may start our criticisms. Is the Weltanschauung of Nietzsche really optimistic? Does he, like Leibniz, think that this world is the best of all possible worlds? Or, if he does not, does he hold that it is possible to make this world the best? If so, how? Is his advice to the human race on the subject of ethics hopeful, or helpful, or depressing?

If we hold fast to the strict philosophical definition of optimism, we shall quickly be able to say that Nietzsche is not an optimist in this sense, for, as we shall soon see (and indeed we have gathered it from earlier chapters in this book), he does not consider this world, as it exists, to be the best of all possible worlds, but nearly the worst: so that strictly speaking he is almost a philosophical pessimist. If we admit the colloquial use of the word, we shall at first be disposed to think that he is an optimist in this sense, for he appears to achievement of the "European" Napoleon. And now they have their Reich, the last word in perverse backwardness, with its Bildungsphilisterei, with Strauss, Wagner, Treitschke—and Bismarck. There is not much hope anywhere: there is no hope at all in Germany. Everything, or almost everything, must go by the board before the human race can again set itself on the upward path, which it left when Socrates and Euripides brought what Hebbel calls "the impulse towards reflection" into the naïve, heroic, inspired older world.

It is not necessary to labour all this, for I do not think that anyone can deny that Nietzsche regards the past development and the present form of civilisation with intense distaste, that he uncompromisingly rejects this world, here and now. This cruel satire and this angry disdain are, incidentally, his most useful service to thought; and for any small progress which we may have made (in some respects) beyond the complacent trivialities of the nineteenth century, we owe a heavy debt of gratitude to Nietzsche—a greater debt than civilisation has ever owed to La Bruyère. All the manifestations of life (says Nietzsche), whatever form they take, are efforts, confused, ignorant, impotent, very likely, but still efforts, *to increase Power*, the power of the living creature concerned. No moral codes or religions or anything else can interfere with this struggle, which is the essential condition of all life: nay more, all moral codes and religions are themselves excellent manifestations of this "Wille zur Macht"—only they tend to increase the power of the wrong people. For it is the priest (that is, in Nietzsche's eyes, the degenerate) and the mob, who profit by ethics and by religion, which enable them to keep the "Raubmenschen" in subjection: and of course it is not desirable to encourage the "Machtwille" of the slaves, but only that of the few *great men*.[1] But whereas the "Macht-

---

[1] The personality of Nietzsche himself was in many ways in striking contrast to that of his "Raubmenschen" or "Übermenschen" (who are, in truth, little more than the "Sturm-und-Drang Kraftkerle"): for Nietzsche was an invalid and a neurotic, solitary, shy, and half-blind, and moreover, a kindly, warm-hearted, if irritable, man in private intercourse. He was also extremely honest and conscientious, scrupulous and, in the ordinary affairs of life,

wille" of the mob, in all its manifestations, must be attacked, repressed, and defeated, that of the great and unscrupulous, the Cesare Borgias, the Napoleons, the Friedrich Hohenstaufens, must have absolutely free play.

If we give free play to the "Machtwille" of the great men, like these, we shall in time produce Supermen. As man is to monkey, so is Superman to man. That is to say, he is the finest type of man—Cesare Borgia, etc.—with all the qualities which make him unusual raised to the nth power; stronger, fiercer, more unscrupulous and cruel and merciless, brave and beautiful and confident, joyous in his own glories, pursuing no ends except his own advantage, treading the rest of the world under his feet just as and when he thinks fit.

The historical characters whom Nietzsche admired—like Cesare Borgia and Napoleon—have been doubtful blessings, and it is questionable if they have greatly contributed to human knowledge, power, beauty, and happiness. It has seemed necessary, for one reason or another, to exercise constraint over their activities, and in the end, as a rule, to cut them short. Nietzsche calls that prejudice and wickedness, saying that they should have had complete liberty: but can we really convince ourselves that he is right? And if the limited activities of the historical "Kraftmenschen" have actually damaged and retarded civilisation (not using the word in the complacent sense of the Reichsdeutsche of 1880, who saw civilisation culminating in themselves, but in the most carefully and *honestly* defined[1] sense which we can

truthful, the last frequently to his own detriment: whereas his "Kraftmensch" would never do anything to his own disadvantage. On the other hand, Nietzsche does possess stubborn and persevering conviction and the greatest mental courage: but this is only half of the "Übermensch", who *must* be physically terrific and exultantly godlike, though he may be a liar, a braggart, and a thief.

[1] When arguing against Nietzsche on this point we cannot connect civilisation with ethical, especially Christian, values, since he regards these as evils. We must rather connect it with beauty, health, strength, art, music, joy, the conquest of mountains and seas, adventure and bravery. If the historical "Kraftmenschen" have aided these and similar things, then they have, according to Nietzsche, promoted civilisation. But in fact they have not advanced these

think of), it would appear that the intensified and uncontrolled "Machtwillen" of intensified hypothetical "Kraftmenschen" (that is "Übermenschen") would soon reduce the world to ruins. One "Machtwille" would be pitted against another, there would be unending war, and competition of every kind, so that no stability could possibly be attained, even for moments. But it takes an act of faith of which most of us are not capable (especially in view of such lessons of history as Athens, the Barbarians and Rome, the Thirty Years' War) to believe that any sort of civilisation can exist, much less improve itself, where there is no stability whatever.

One is then doubtful as to the excellence of the results which will be obtained by breeding Nietzsche's Supermen. One has suspicions that such a process may result in race suicide, or in the retrogression of such civilisation as the world has reached, with all its imperfections and perversions, to a condition of mere primitive animalism. The result of war upon mental, moral and physical standards is bound to be bad. The Thirty Years' War, for example, worked unutterable damage upon every side of German civilisation, and in the modern world, since the use of firearms, war does not mean the survival of the physically finest. And on that point at least, chaos and war and violence would defeat Nietzsche's objects: for however ambiguous, varying, and inconsistent may be his different definitions of his Supermen, there is one point on which he is perfectly clear and perfectly consistent— the Superman will be physically perfect. He will be attained by breeding from the strongest, largest, most beautiful existing men. And of course, conversely, the weak and unhealthy and ugly ought to—*must*—be degraded, oppressed, and finally annihilated. But the world will not bring about these results, any more than it will improve the intellectual

---

things, and therefore Nietzsche, like most people, only for different reasons (the reason of most people being the disregard of such men for ethical laws), ought logically to condemn them. And surely Supermen—that is to say "Kraftmenschen" vastly intensified— would do still less to promote these (genuinely) *civilised* ends?

level of some men or all men (for it is not clear which Nietzsche desires thus to raise), by producing a state of continual upheaval and insecurity, or by intensifying competition too much.[1]

On the practical side, then, Nietzsche's ideals are a counsel of despair, which will bring about the degradation or extermination of man, not his improvement; and it now appears doubtful whether we ought to call him an optimist even in the second, vulgarised sense of the word.

But let us suppose that somehow or other these difficulties have been overcome, that Nietzsche's ideal society has been attained, that it is indeed as perfect as his expectations—what then? What fresh achievements, what new conquests shall attract the Superman, as he stands, lonely, splendid and terrible, brooding over the ruins of our degenerate age, which he has destroyed in his upward struggle? The prophet, who has foretold and longed for this day, this race, will surely have seen, dimly perhaps, but confidently, some further vision of his ideal being penetrating beyond and above, not resting on what he has already reached? For what nobler, greater, more dreadful goal, faintly portended, hotly desired, will be the next endeavour?

We have seen already that in fact Nietzsche gives us no such dim exciting vision: he presents us with a definite deliberate statement of the further fate of man, and nothing more miserable could well be imagined. No further progress can take place: the world must go back to the beginning and go through identically the same course again. Man will start

[1] Nietzsche is not generally concerned with Economics or Industry: but even before he went mad in 1888 it was possible to observe in the shipping industry and on railways that ordinary competition led to the growth, by absorption and amalgamation, of several large concerns, whose attempts to dominate the industry led to a phase of acute and most unprofitable strife. Finally agreements had to be made between the competing firms, to render it possible for them to carry on at all. It seems impossible that the human race can be improved, in the ways in which Nietzsche desired to improve it, by that sort of cut-throat competition. The Industrial Revolution has not made men physically stronger or more beautiful, though no doubt it has sharpened their wits.

with—whatever he originally started with: he will go through exactly the same evolution, general and particular; the same individuals will perform the same acts in the same relation to one another, and the Superman will again be attained. And so on *ad infinitum*. Progress is not an ascending line, but a circle: necessity rules all things: there is no ground for excitement, no possibility of hope.

I believe that Recurrence is more significant than any other of Nietzsche's ideas, more characteristic and more explanatory of the inner workings of his mind. Certainly, in regard to our present investigation, there is no more important point in Nietzsche's teaching: together with the closely con-nected Dionysus-philosophy, "Wiederkehr" seems to be the strongest argument in support of the contention that Nietzsche's philosophy is really a philosophy of despair and gloom: and, what is more, these two closely related theories serve as a bridge between our propositions, and lead us naturally to consider the argument that Nietzsche was from time to time insincere, and more sceptical in his mind than in his writings.

I do not desire to repeat more than I am forced of Nietzsche's various utterances on the subject of "Wieder-kehr": but a certain amount of repetition there will have to be. Let us therefore recall to our minds that Nietzsche does not make the theory his own until *Also sprach Zarathustra*, though he had referred to the existence or possibility of such a belief in more than one passage in his earlier works (and incidentally, in the references of his undoubtedly optimistic but transitory second period, had shown the natural reaction of a cheerful mind to the idea of a cyclic universe, namely horror, amazement, or scorn). But when he puts the theory forward as his own in *Zarathustra*, he does so for the only reasons which he can urge with any validity (reasons which had already occurred to him in the famous passage at the end of *Die fröhliche Wissenschaft*). These reasons are: (*a*) Re-currence is a belief which is intolerable to all except the strongest; (*b*) to the strongest it is "the highest formula of asseveration, which can be attained at all". Therefore it is the centre, the most important, of all the doctrines of *Zara-thustra* (the fundamental conception of the work) and it is just as necessary to all the works of elaboration which follow *Zarathustra*.

It is here important for us to notice: (*a*) that Nietzsche calls his belief hopeful and encouraging—"highest formula of asseveration"; (*b*) that other people, when commenting on his work, have not criticised the term; and (*c*) the arguments which he uses. For as soon as we approach the problem with a mind unprejudiced in regard to (*a*), we shall find ourselves looking very askance at the arguments: we shall soon begin to feel that Recurrence is hopeless, gloomy, and dull. Let us try to summarise once more the reasoning which Nietzsche employs.

It is desirable, he says, to make man "stronger, more malicious, deeper, and more beautiful", in other words, to raise him to Superman, but it is far more desirable if he is to return eternally and to go through all the same stages of development. Conversely, it is all the more necessary to progress to the Superman, in order to have a being great and strong and joyous enough to desire the infinite recurrence of his own life. It is necessary "to create a being, which can bear this teaching". The only being who will not only bear it but welcome it is the Superman. "Zarathustra tells from out of the joy of the Superman the secret, that everything recurs." Moreover, the mere belief in Eternal Recurrence will help to produce the Superman and get rid of the weak.

The great disciplining thought, a hammer in the hand of the mightiest man, with which he smashes degenerating and dying races, and thrusts them out of the way, in order to make space for a new ordering of life, or in order to give to that which is degenerate and desires to die out, a longing for its end.

The men who will be able to bear and to welcome the thought are:

The strongest, the most moderate, those who do not need any extreme articles of belief, those who not only admit a good deal of chance and senselessness, but like it; those who can think of man with a considerable moderation of his value, without thereby becoming small and weak: the richest in health, who are equal to most

"malheurs", and are therefore not so frightened of those "malheurs"
—men who are certain of their power, and who, with conscious
pride, represent the highest attained power of humanity.

Such, of course, are the only men whom Nietzsche will
encourage.

Then, to remind ourselves again of all the consequences of
the idea, and its full importance, let us repeat a passage from
the *Wille zur Macht* fragments.

Such an experimental philosophy, as I teach, tentatively anticipates even the possibilities of the most thorough-going Nihilism:
by which I do not mean that it would remain stationary at a negation,
at a "No", at the will to say "No". Rather it will go through as far
as the very opposite—as far as a Dionysiac asseveration of the world,
as it is, without reduction, exception, or selection—it desires the
eternal *circular course*: the same things, the same logicality and
illogicality of association. Highest state which a philosopher can
reach: to stand Dionysiacally to existence: my formula for it is
amor fati.[1]

It is similarly necessary to value less highly the side of existence
which hitherto has alone been accepted; to comprehend, whence
this acceptance originates and *how little it is applicable to a Dionysiac
estimation of existence*: I extracted and understood that which really
says "Yes" here (on the one side the instinct of the sufferers, on the
other side the instinct of the herd, and that third instinct, that of the
majority against the exceptions).

Therewith I guessed to what extent a stronger sort of man must
necessarily devise for himself, in another direction, the *elevation*
and magnification of man: *higher beings* as beyond good and evil, as
beyond those values which cannot deny their origin from the sphere
of suffering, of the herd, and of the majority—I sought for the
onset of the inverted formation of ideals in history (the concepts
"heathen", "classical", "noble", rediscovered and set up).

This is all fairly straightforward, and we shall be justified
in saying that Nietzsche regards the theory of Recurrence
both as a reason and as a consequence of the Superman—a
circular argument—and that he considers, too, that the
acceptance of such a belief will prove fatal to the weak creatures of whom he desires to be rid. I carefully say "acceptance", not *truth*, because there is no indication, until *Der
Wille zur Macht*, that Nietzsche either believed, or tried to
prove, Recurrence *as true*. He puts it forward like the

[1] An instructive remark.

Hesiodic Muse, as a belief which it is *good for men to hold*. Yes, for his own particular type of men. In *Der Wille zur Macht* he does try to prove, logically and scientifically, that it is true. One feels that he is there trying to force himself to believe as an afterthought, or as a desperate effort to overcome a doubt: and one cannot see that there is any logic or any science in his proof.

We have already examined this proof in some detail, and we have concluded that it is quite untenable, for, among a variety of other sins, it appears to contradict the second law of thermodynamics, and therefore, it seems, there is no hope for it. We cannot, however, blame Nietzsche for not anticipating recent physical knowledge (though I suppose we can justly blame him for not knowing enough about the science of his own day): but we can and do condemn him for his casual, vague, half-hearted reasoning. For even if we allow him to say, in the way he does, off-hand and dogmatically, that a creation is impossible (which cannot be logically proved), even then the arguments which he bases upon this unsatisfactory hypothesis are very weak, even for Nietzsche, who was a poet, a man of instinct, a brilliant guesser, but a very poor reasoner.

And with this attempted proof he leaves us. He never completed *Der Wille zur Macht*: he never added anything to these unsatisfactory sections, but it is not easy to see how anything reasonable could have been worked out on those lines. Indeed I am inclined to regard this whole business of logically elaborating *Zarathustra* with a somewhat sceptical eye; especially this part of that work. Frequently one finds Nietzsche taking the most pains over the things which he least believed; and all this careful justification of the fine poetry, in which Zarathustra speaks of Recurrence, seems a little thin, unless it is to conceal something, such as a doubt, struggling to get to the surface, while Nietzsche is struggling to keep it down.

This, however, we can leave unsettled. We will discuss the matter of Nietzsche's doubts a little later. But I think we must all admit that Recurrence is a gloomy prospect for most of us, and that Nietzsche meant it so to be. It seems dull, unenterprising, undignified, and it makes life purposeless. Nietzsche often betrays—sometimes he claims—a kinship with Eastern fatalism, and we recall that in some of the passages about Recurrence he praises the fatalism which such a belief will encourage.

Whatever each individual imagines, the other will let it stand.... He to whom effort gives the highest feelings, let him exert effort; he to whom rest gives the highest feelings, let him rest; he to whom discipline, submission, obedience give the highest feelings, let him obey.

But fatalism would be a denial of all that Nietzsche usually professes to stand for, and to convict him of it would mean revaluing his work from beginning to end. We will not try to make out that he is a Nirvanist, but we will leave the theory of Eternal Recurrence with a growing doubt about the joyous hopefulness of his philosophy. We are by now agreed, I hope, that this part of the system looks more like a confession of weakness, a confession that he lacks a satisfactory aim or end. If we go on long enough we may yet find ourselves calling him a sceptic.

The whole business is really summed up in Nietzsche's description of his system as "Philosophie des Dionysos" and of himself as "the last disciple of the philosopher Dionysus, the teacher of Eternal Recurrence". The idea of Recurrence and the idea of Dionysiasm are brought into close contact by this sentence, just as they are closely connected in Nietzsche's philosophy.

Again I do not desire or need to revert at any length to a subject which I have already treated pretty fully. I only require to summarise briefly once more some of the main conclusions which have been reached concerning "the philosophy of Dionysus", and to try to relate these conclusions to our present investigation.

"A Dionysiac view of life" is the philosophy, essentially pessimistic, of the man who sees at the root of existence things strange, terrible, and perhaps fatal, who sees that great wisdom only brings great disaster, that the more man knows, the more he will suffer, that the universe is not made or guided by a kindly or beneficent power. But it is a philosophy which accepts all that. Seeing the evil, pain, and terror, it says "yes" to life *as it is*, not as optimistic religion or decorative art, the art of Apollo, represents it. From Intoxication, the gift of Dionysus, comes the greatness, the strength, the power, to overcome and to accept, and in Lyricism, Intoxication, Exaltation is the salvation of man.

The Dionysiac view of life involves:

The affirmative answer to life even in its strangest and hardest problems; the will to life, rejoicing, in the *sacrifice* of its highest types, at its own inexhaustible nature—*that* I called Dionysiac, that I understood as a bridge to the psychology of the *tragic* poet. *Not* in order to rid oneself of pity and fear, not in order to purge oneself of a dangerous emotion through an unrestrained release —Aristotle misunderstood it in this sense: but actually to be, far beyond pity and fear, the eternal joy of Becoming—that joy which also includes the joy in *Destroying*.

Nietzsche continues this same passage with the comment: "In this sense I have the right to understand myself as the first tragic philosopher—that is to say, the extremest contrast and antipode of a pessimistic philosopher".

I do not think that we ought to be in any hurry to accept this contradistinction of "pessimistic" and "tragic". We must remember that Nietzsche has already set tragic drama and optimistic philosophy—Socrates—in the sharpest possible opposition;[1] and we find it difficult, on Nietzsche's bare assertion, to oppose Pessimism and Tragedy in this way. Of course, in a sense it is true that Dionysiac inspiration will produce delirious intoxicated ecstasy, unification with the "Weltall", oblivion or disregard of the final terrors—but it is the happiness of the drunken bankrupt, not of the philosopher, and the awakening is bound to come before long. Let us repeat a famous passage.

Either through the influence of the narcotic drink, about which all primeval men and peoples speak in songs, or at the mighty onset of Spring, which permeates all nature with desire, awake those Dionysiac stirrings, in whose climax all that is subjective vanishes

[1] In *Die Geburt der Tragödie*, from which this passage is an extract.

in complete self-forgetfulness.... Not only, under the spell of Dionysiasm, is the bond between man and man joined up again: Nature too, alienated, hostile, or subjected, celebrates again her feast of reconciliation with her lost son, Man. Of its own free will the earth offers its gifts, and peaceably the beasts of prey of the rocks and the wilderness draw near. With flowers and garlands is the car of Dionysus loaded: under his yoke walk panther and tiger. Change Beethoven's triumphal Song of Joy into a picture, and be not behindhand with your imagination, when the millions sink in awe into the dust: so you can approach Dionysiasm. Now the slave is a free man, now are shattered all the rigid, hostile barriers, which need, whim, or insolent fashion has set up between men. Now, hearing the gospel of universal harmony, each feels himself not only united with his neighbour, reconciled, blended, but One, as if the veil of Maya were torn up, and only fluttered now in rags before the mysterious Original Unity. Singing and dancing, man expresses himself as member of a higher community: he has un-learnt walking and speaking, and is on the way to fly up into the air as he dances. Enchantment speaks from his gestures...he feels himself like a god, he himself moves now as enraptured and uplifted, just as in his dreams he saw the gods move. Man is no longer an artist, he has become a work of art: all the artistic powers of nature, to the highest ecstatic satisfaction of the Original Unity, reveal themselves here in the thrills of intoxication. The noblest clay, the most precious marble—man—is moulded and hewn here, and to the chisel-strokes of the Dionysiac maker of worlds resounds the cry of the Eleusinian mysteries: "Ye bow down, millions? Dost thou suspect thy creator, O world?"

This is very fine, inspired, full of excitement, rhythm, and ecstasy: but it is a dream. It is a momentary, transient paradise, an instant of peace and reconciliation in a world whose normal state is terror and war. Dionysus is no eternal god, no controller of the awful mysteries, but a magician, whose gifts can for a minute intoxicate the fugitive creatures of earth, making them forget their destiny and feel them-selves—by illusion—one with the laws of life. But his magic cannot endure: the realities remain, black, relentless, terrible: when the Dionysiac comes round from his ecstatic swoon he will say again: "Not to be born is the best fate of all: but if a man be born, it is much better that he return whence he came as quickly as possible".

But this is not all. There is a more practical side to Dionysiac philosophy. Belief in Dionysus, acceptance of that view of things, will have a definite traceable effect upon men. It will help them on the way to being Supermen, for Dionysus, though he is a god, is also a Superman. The most important change will be that the follower of Dionysus, like his master, will become hard, ruthless, cruel, and very strong. He will be able (thanks to his power of self-intoxication) to bear everything, and there is nothing that he will fear or hesitate to do.

He who is most rich in fullness of life, the Dionysiac god and man, can not only permit himself to see what is frightful and questionable, but can even permit himself frightful actions and every luxury of destruction, disintegration, denial; where he is concerned, that which is evil, senseless, and ugly seems, so to speak, permitted, as it seems permitted in nature, in consequence of an excess of creative, restorative powers, which is able to make a luxuriant land of fruit out of any desert.

He is strong enough to accept all pain, sorrow, cruelty. "He says 'yes' to even the sharpest suffering: he is strong enough, full enough, deifier enough to do so", and to those weaker than himself he is as hard as a diamond.

But such a philosophy has little attraction or hope for us. It is a doctrine of despair for all except the very few—Supermen, or whatever one may call them—who are great enough, savage enough, self-sufficient enough, to accept things as they are, based upon intolerable *profunda*—perhaps because they can make sure that the pain and sorrow, which are inevitable, are borne, not by themselves, but by their weaker neighbours. But leaving aside these problematical demi-gods, what has Nietzsche's Weltanschauung to offer us, who are not Supermen, nor aspire to be? Nothing at all, except the alternative prospects of continuing to mismanage the world just as, God knows, we are doing to-day, or of submitting, unconditionally and for ever, to the unchecked dominance of the Superman, who will be a hard master, and a master who serves no end but his own. And, after all, our submission and our slavery will lead to nothing—no better future or higher race, not even for our masters. It will simply end in a return to the very beginning from which humanity will again and again have to tread the same way of sorrow, all to no purpose. And when we review this in our minds and especially when we remember that from first to last Nietzsche insists "that the deepest wisdom is an abomination contrary to nature", that the foundations of life are awful beyond endurance, are we not justified in refusing to believe that he preached a philosophy of joyous hopefulness?

I mentioned just now that Nietzsche's apparent belief in his own mission may not really be sincere, that he was often afflicted by doubts about the possibility or even desirability of reaching his future ideal civilisation. I then remarked, while momentarily deferring discussion of the matter, that it was a difficult subject, on which certainty could hardly be attained: but let us now see what can be made of it.

We shall have to seek our evidence in what one may call the "asides", moments of unguarded self-revelation, of which there are quite a large number.[1] But before we go on to this, it may be as well to remind ourselves, very briefly, about certain facts concerning Nietzsche's career.

Let us remember that there have been few writers who have worked under greater difficulties. He was ill (often violently ill) more days than he was well. He was nearly blind at the age of thirty-five: he was lonely, unpopular, unsuccessful, poor: no one understood him, and no one was interested in his work: he had every reason to believe that he had completely failed: finally he went mad. We may well wonder that this sickly outcast could have held an ardent and continual belief in the fundamental excellence of life: we may reasonably begin by being a little suspicious of his good faith when he calls himself an optimist.

But this is tending to beg the whole question, and we had better proceed at once to unearth the above-mentioned "asides". They can, I think, be conveniently and logically divided under three headings:

(1) Some of the poems and *Zarathustra*.

(2) *Ecce homo*.

[1] As one would expect with an author who suddenly went mad while at the height of his activity, and who therefore left a considerable mass of plans, sketches, notes, etc., largely not intended for publication, to be gone through and collected by others.

(3) Some of Nietzsche's comments, at various times and in
various places, on Socrates.

Investigating these last will involve repeating some of what I
have said already, but not very much.

In the poems it is not difficult to find a good deal of what
seems like Romantic "Sehnsucht", unfulfilled, hopeless
longing, and Romantic unbelief in the mission or success of
the singer (of course a large number of Nietzsche's poems are
epigrams or sneers, but I leave those entirely out of consideration). They are often—I will not say "generally"—
rather sad poems, very far in spirit from the desperate pro-
vocativeness of most of Nietzsche's prose. For instance, the
well-known poem entitled "Venedig":[1]

> An der Brücke stand
> jüngst ich in brauner Nacht.
> Fernher kam Gesang:
> goldner Tropfen quoll's
> über die zitternde Fläche weg.
> Gondeln, Lichter, Musik,
> trunken schwamm's in die Dämmrung hinaus....
> Meine Seele, ein Saitenspiel,
> sang sich, unsichtbar berührt,
> heimlich ein Gondellied dazu,
> zitternd vor bunter Seligkeit.
> ......Hörte jemand ihr zu?...[2]

At first the music is not in the poet's own soul: the night
is not glorious, but melancholy brown; the song comes from
afar, and he only echoes it. He is not amidst the merriment
and the music, he merely reflects it, and his quick sensibility
soon takes it up, adopts, imagines the "bright joyousness" of
the singers. But then, at once, comes the return to reality,
to the loneliness and ineffectiveness and neglect of the poet's

[1] This poem is a product of one of Nietzsche's last hours of
sanity. He was heard singing it in the train while he was being
brought home, mad, from Turin.

[2] "I stood by the bridge, very recently, in brown night. From far
away came song: in golden drops it swelled away over the quivering
surface. Gondolas, lights, music, drunken they floated out into the
twilight....My soul, the play of strings, invisibly moved, secretly
sang itself a gondola-song thereto, quivering with bright joyousness....Was anyone listening to it?..."

own life—"Was anyone listening to it?"—No, no one was listening: the song might just as well have been unrepeated: the distant revellers and the near night are all inattentive: the poet is still alone, and knows that he is alone.

This loneliness he expressed more directly, though also more defiantly, in the lines "Pinie und Blitz":

> Hoch wuchs ich über Mensch und Tier;
> Und sprech' ich—Niemand spricht mit mir
> Zu einsam wuchs ich und zu hoch—
> Ich warte: worauf wart' ich doch?
> Zu nah ist mir der Wolken Sitz—
> Ich warte auf den nächsten Blitz.[1]

Here, at any rate, the poet possesses the clearest possible foreknowledge of the fate in store for him, and has no sanguine self-delusions about his place in life. He seems himself pre-doomed to be a sacrifice to the cruel elemental powers. He has sinned against them, broken their command, $\mu\eta\delta\grave{\epsilon}\nu$ $\check{\alpha}\gamma\alpha\nu$, but they will be avenged in their own time.

Another excellent example of the melancholy longing of Nietzsche's poetry is the poem "Der Wanderer". One ought to say, in reference to this, that Nietzsche continually (and most aptly) characterises himself as a "wanderer": for example in "Der Wanderer und sein Schatten", and over and over again in *Zarathustra*: so that there is every reason to regard the poem as subjective, and to treat it as a confession or self-revelation. It runs as follows:

> Es geht ein Wandrer durch die Nacht
> Mit gutem Schritt;
> Und krummes Tal und lange Höhn—
> Er nimmt sie mit—
> Die Nacht ist schön—
> Er schreitet zu und steht nicht still,
> Weiss nicht, wohin sein Weg noch will.

[1] "High I grew above man and animal; and if I speak, no one speaks with me.

"Too lonely I grew and too high—I wait: but for what am I waiting?

"Too near to me is the home of the clouds—I wait for the next flash of lightning."

Da singt ein Vogel durch die Nacht:
"Ach Vogel, was hast du gemacht!
Was hemmst du meinen Sinn und Fuss
Und giessest süssen Herz-Verdruss
In's Ohr mir, dass ich stehen muss
Und lauschen muss—
Was *lockst* du mich mit Ton und Gruss?"

Der gute Vogel schweigt und spricht:
"Nein, Wanderer, nein! Dich lock' ich nicht
Mit dem Getön—
Ein Weibchen lock' ich von den Höhn—
Was geht's dich an?
Allein ist mir die Nacht nicht schön—
Was geht's dich an? Denn du sollst gehn
Und nimmer, nimmer, stille stehn!
Was stehst du noch?
Was tat mein Flötenlied dir an,
Du Wandersmann?"

.   .   .   .   .   .

Der gute Vogel schwieg und sann:
"Was tat mein Flötenlied ihm an?
Was steht er noch?—
Der arme, arme Wandersmann!"[1]

I do not say that this kind of "Sehnsucht" in the poems can be used to prove more than moments—passing moments, perhaps—of sadness, melancholy, regret, in Nietzsche himself: but I do think that the existence of these pieces shows

---

[1] "There goes a wanderer through the night, stepping out bravely; and twisting valley and long ridges—he takes them as they come: the night is beautiful—he steps ahead and stands not still, knows not, whither his way still tends.

"Then a bird sings through the night: 'O bird, what hast thou done! Why dost thou stay my mind and foot, and pourest into my ear sweet misery of the heart, that I must stand and listen: why dost thou *entice* me with song and greeting?'

"The good bird is silent, then he speaks: 'Nay, wanderer, nay! Thee I do not entice with my song: I am calling a mate from the heights—what does it concern thee? If I am alone the night is not fair to me—what does it concern thee? For thou must go on, and never, never stand still! Why standest thou yet? What did my flute-song to thee, thou wanderer?'

.   .   .   .

"The good bird was silent, and thought: 'What did my flute-song to him? Why stands he yet?—The poor, poor wanderer!'"

that he had such moments. And after all they are not un-
common or insignificant. There are many such poems, which,
as poetry, are by no means contemptible. Nor are these
moments confined to one particular period of his poetry. The
instances thus far given are all from poems of the years
1882-5: but in the Dionysus-dithyrambs of 1888—"The
songs of Zarathustra, which he sang to himself, in order that
he might bear his last loneliness"—there are many flashes of
the same mood:

> So sank ich selber einstmals
> aus meinem Wahrheits-Wahnsinne,
> aus meinen Tages-Sehnsüchten,
> des Tages müde, krank vom Lichte,
> —sank abwärts, abendwärts, schattenwärts,
> von einer Wahrheit
> verbrannt und durstig
> —gedenkst du noch, gedenkst du, heisses Herz,
> wie da du durstetest?—
> *dass ich verbannt sei*
> *von aller Wahrheit!*
> Nur Narr! Nur Dichter![1]

The two italicised lines are particularly significant,
especially in view of evidence to which we shall come later.

Loneliness is the constant *motif* of these poems, as it is of
Zarathustra itself, the seventh loneliness of the prophet, who
knows so much more than ordinary men that he cannot
associate with them nor reveal to them more than a tiny
fraction of his wisdom: so that he must go on alone, bearing
alone and unshared this terrible burden of knowledge:

> Bleib stark, mein tapfres Herz:
> Frag nicht: warum?[2]

Excellent and characteristic is the scene in the fourth book of
Zarathustra, called "Der Zauberer", with the verses:

---

[1] "So sank I once myself, from my truth-madness, from my
longings for day, weary of the day, sick from the light—sank downwards, towards the evening, towards the shadows, burned and
thirsty with a truth:—dost thou remember still, dost thou
remember, my burning heart, how thou didst thirst there?—*that I
was banned from all truth!* Only a fool, only a poet!"

[2] "Remain strong, my brave heart: ask not, 'Why?'"

Wer wärmt mich, wer liebt mich noch?
Gebt heisse Hände!
Gebt Herzens-Kohlenbecken!
Hingestreckt, schaudernd,
Halbtodtem gleich, dem man die Füsse wärmt—
Geschüttelt, ach! von unbekannten Fiebern,
Zitternd vor spitzen eisigen Frost-Pfeilern,
Von dir gejagt, Gedanke!
Unnennbarer! Verhüllter! Entsetzlicher!
Du Jäger hinter Wolken!...
.....................................gequält
Von allen ewigen Martern,
Du unbekannter—Gott!...[1]

This is not put into the mouth of Zarathustra, but of his adversary, Der Zauberer: and yet, how characteristic of Nietzsche it is to personify himself, partly at least, in each of two contrasted persons. How often in his early works, when he speaks of Schopenhauer or Wagner,[2] does he refer, really, to himself: and how typical it is of his attitude to his adversaries when he says, in *Zarathustra*: "Here are priests: and even if they are my enemies, I beg you to pass them by quietly and with sheathed sword: for my blood is akin to theirs, and I desire to know that my blood is honoured in theirs...". I do not think that there is much doubt that in the "old magician", just as in the other types and personages whom Nietzsche assaults, there is almost as much of the philosopher's own self as there is in Zarathustra.

[1] "Who warms me, who loves me still? Give me warm hands, give me the stores of coal of your hearts! Stretched out I lie, shuddering, like to a half-dead man, whose feet one warms—shaken, ah, by unknown fevers, trembling for sharp icy arrows of frost, hunted by thee, O thought, unnamable one, hidden one, terrible one! Thou hunter behind clouds!...tormented by all eternal torments, thou unknown—God!..."

[2] I do not believe all that Nietzsche says about this in *Ecce homo*: "*Whenever* in my early books I spoke of Wagner or Schopenhauer, I meant myself". That is the kind of exaggeration which is typical of *Ecce homo*. But at least it is partly true. There is reliable evidence of this kind of thing in many other places. We know that Nietzsche sometimes revolted against himself, or some of himself, and that he therefore invested his *bêtes noires* with some of his own characteristics.

So much for the evidence of the poems and *Zarathustra*. They suggest a deeper and more frequent feeling of dissatisfaction, longing, loneliness, disbelief in his own mission, than we have been accustomed to look for in Nietzsche. Let us go on to *Ecce homo*, the most self-revealing of all his works, and see whether, thence also, similar evidence may not be obtained.

There is much, in the beginning of *Ecce homo*, about decadence, much about Nietzsche's own symptoms, diseases, weaknesses: all of which reveals a very clear eye for that side of his life. "A long, all too long series of years unfortunately means also at the same time retrogression, decay, periodicity of a sort of decadence. Do I need, after all that, to say that in questions of decadence I am *experienced*?" On the other hand: "Apart from the fact that I am a decadent, I am also its opposite". His insistence upon this last statement is perhaps a little suspicious. "It was in the years of my lowest vitality that I *ceased* to be a pessimist", he says, and so on: but it is especially valuable for our present purpose to observe how clearly and repeatedly Nietzsche tells us that he abandoned pessimism, the natural standpoint for an invalid, *by an act of will*, and that his optimism is *forced*.

Proceeding a little farther with this book, we shall find some interesting, and, though incidental, significant remarks about scepticism and cynicism—"The Sceptics, the only *honourable* type among the race of philosophers, who are usually so ambiguous or quinquebiguous"; and later on: "Here and there...my books attain the highest thing which can be reached on earth, namely cynicism". Such remarks have appeared in other places in Nietzsche's works, but it is particularly interesting to find them in this, his "Confessions". Does he really set such a very high value on scepticism or cynicism? One would not have thought it from his other works. May one indulge for a moment in a suspicion that after all the man himself may be a sceptic or a cynic? Let us put the suspicion hastily on one side.

But it is not for these individual instances of peculiar and unexpected tendencies of thought (there are a very great number of them) that *Ecce homo* is so valuable. It is rather because of the general tone of the book, which immediately strikes any reader (and probably disgusts him) without being at all easy to analyse. Nor, after a good deal of study, do I feel at all confident that I have made out what is at the bottom of it all. But it seems it is something like this. Nietzsche sees that he is quite unsuccessful, still unheeded, still ill and lonely: he finds his sensibilities becoming more and more overstrained by life, as it meets him (that is clearly shown by the very odd harsh note of the books immediately before *Ecce homo*), and he has begun to doubt, seriously, whether after all he is on the right track. Like most people he has had momentary doubts at various times before, but the doubt has by now become far more persistent and disturbing. What is to be done about it? One cannot feel like that when one is on the eve of writing one's masterpiece (*Der Wille zur Macht*): it is no use trying to write the masterpiece when one perhaps does not believe in it any more. Very well, then, let us sit down and think it out clearly, and perhaps we shall get our mind straight, and be rid of our doubts. Let us do it in the form of an autobiography, in which, before all else, we will *analyse* our experiences, difficulties, character, and past generally: and hence attain clearness about our opinions and the books in which we have expressed them: so that at the end we may have analysed away our present distress, and cleared our mind, and we can say, before we set out upon our most formidable, crowning task, "now we have settled with the past: farewell to all those troubles".

But the outstanding feature of the autobiography is that it does not lay *one* of the spectres. That is probably the real reason for the peculiarity of *Ecce homo*. It does not get straight to grips with any of these troubles. It goes round them, lunges at them, and then retires, and above all—the surest sign of an unconvinced mind—it protests too much, like the Player Queen in *Hamlet*. The first paragraph is an excellent example of this.

In the foreknowledge that I must soon approach humanity with the hardest demand which has ever been put to it, it seems to me essential to say *who I am*. Fundamentally people ought to know that, for I have not "left myself untestified". But the lack of proportion between the greatness of my task and the *smallness* of my contemporaries has found expression in the fact that people have neither heard me nor even seen me.... In these circumstances there is a duty, against which at bottom my habit, and much more the pride of my instincts, revolts, namely to say: "*Hear me! For I am he and he. Above all else do not confuse me with another!*"

This tone is maintained all through the book. Measureless self-exaltation, measureless disparagement of those who differ from him, just as in the books since *Zarathustra*, only naïver, shriller, *uneasier*. Nothing convinces in *Ecce homo*, though it is full of enlightening phrases and interesting, self-revealing criticism of Nietzsche's life and works: a desperate attempt to deny that he is German by race, or that he is infected in any way with the plague of German pessimism and "unculture", a furious effort to show that he really never praised Wagner or Schopenhauer, but that when he spoke of them, in his early books, he *always* meant himself: and much more of the same kind: the tone getting wilder and wilder, almost incoherent at the end, where, as usual, Nietzsche has got on to his *bête noire*, Christianity: "Have people understood me?—Dionysus against the Crucified...".

It is all very interesting, very instructive, and entirely unconvincing, and if, as I believe, Nietzsche deliberately and carefully set out to overcome his own doubts, and to convince himself, he could not possibly have succeeded. He has only worked himself into a state of wild excitement.

It is to my mind extremely significant, in this connection, that the most striking saying, concerning the philosopher's disbelief in his own mission, occurs in *Der Wille zur Macht*. Did this disbelief, not exorcised by *Ecce homo*, increase and dominate? Did it contribute to Nietzsche's sudden madness?

Many of the most remarkable instances of Nietzsche's apparent waverings, doubts, and self-rejections, are best discussed under the general heading of his extremely important relationship to Socrates. But it would be well before entering into this problem to remind ourselves of an extremely important point—it comes again in connection with Socrates: indeed the whole Socrates-argument culminates in something very similar—namely, the thoroughly Greek attitude of Nietzsche, shown primarily in respect of the Dionysus cult, secondarily in respect of knowledge in general, about *not knowing too much*.

We shall find this in *Ecce homo* more than once: "How much truth does a spirit dare, how much truth does it stand?" he asks, as one of the most important questions concerning any man; and clearer still: "Do people *understand* Hamlet? It is not doubt, but *certainty*, which makes a man mad...but one must be deep, abysmal, a philosopher, to feel so....We are all *afraid* of Truth...".

But this does not only occur in *Ecce homo*. Over and over again, especially in the poems, we can find the same thing.

> Still!
> Von grossen Dingen,—ich sehe Grosses!
> Soll man schweigen
> Oder gross reden:
> Rede gross, meine entzückte Weisheit![1]

You must not know too much: you must not guess too well; clear vision is a crime against the world-order. That is the deepest secret of the worship of Dionysus, and it comes out (as we have seen before) in nearly all of Nietzsche's works.

There is no room for doubt about the *reason* for this precept of silence. The fundamental realities which knowledge will reveal are too dreadful to be borne—we have seen that before when we discussed Dionysiac philosophy. Yet we also find a number of instances when Nietzsche no longer opposes the dreadfulness with Dionysiac courage, will to identification, intoxication, but takes refuge in silence, in an obstinate refusal to let the truth escape. These are only moments, of course, but they are moments fairly widely scattered in his life, from 1871 to 1888. And it seems impossible to avoid the conclusion that at such moments Nietzsche sees his deepest thoughts as black and dangerous, that he despairs, wavers, and—holds his tongue; partly, I

---

[1] "Be silent! About great things,—I see something great! one must keep silent, or speak great words: speak great words, my entranced wisdom!"

suppose, because he doubts whether the ordinary run of men are great enough to endure the philosophy of Dionysus, partly too, because in these moments of vision he knows and feels that it is a philosophy of black pessimism and hopeless despair.

Let us now pass on to our particular aspect of the Socratic question.

We have already discussed some general aspects of this question, and we will repeat as little as possible. Let us remind ourselves, first of all, that in the first and third of his clearly defined stages of development Nietzsche detests Socrates, while in the second stage he deeply admires him. If we look back to Chapter III, we shall find all the evidence we require, both as to the intensity of Nietzsche's feelings of hatred or admiration, and as to the reasons which he alleges. It is clear enough that Nietzsche dislikes Socrates more often than he likes him, and more vehemently: but the very vehemence of the dislike, the immoderateness of the criticism, and the fertility of Nietzsche in providing new reasons for condemning Socrates, are grounds for suspicion; suspicion, that is, of some other motive, never, or not clearly, avowed, but very powerful, in Nietzsche's hatred; a motive which, if we can discover it, will give us a deeper insight into the workings of Nietzsche's mind.

Very likely Socrates was the kind of person of whom Nietzsche disapproves in principle, that is to say, a theorist, a moralist, a level-headed bourgeois. But that alone would not be enough to explain the ferocious intensity of Nietzsche's antagonism. We must call upon an explanation which we have met before—namely self-identification. Nietzsche's hatred reaches its climax because (1) he disapproves of Socrates, (2) he feels that he is *very like him*.

No doubt he is right: and that is one of the strongest possible arguments in support of my second proposition. Socrates *is* the antithesis of what Nietzsche desired to be; Socrates' teaching *is* the contradiction of Zarathustra's. Every time that Nietzsche sees a resemblance, in himself, to Socrates, he sees a weakness in his own position; and every time that he speaks harshly of Socrates, he is speaking in an irritation caused by his own misgivings, which he cannot avoid. His belief in his own philosophy is weakened by knowing how near he is to its antithesis.

But Nietzsche not only *felt* that he was like Socrates: he *was* like Socrates. In no way was he more like him, as we have seen already, than in the ideal of being a *teacher*. That this was a Socratic ideal, I need hardly argue; for if one thing is made plain by nearly every word which we read about Socrates, it is that he was first, last, and all the time, a teacher of men, especially of young men. The same is true of Nietzsche, although various factors have combined to hide it from students. We tend to see in Nietzsche the scientific philosopher, the "Freigeist", the anti-Christian, the artist, the psychologist, the poet, and so on: but we can see just as clearly, if we look, the would-be teacher, from the time when Nietzsche became professor at Basel, until the time when he went mad, partly because there was no prospect of ever attaining his ends.

But there are several other important points in which Nietzsche resembles Socrates, and these, too, we had better run through briefly. Let us remember that the ἔρως of Platonic dialogue is found in the Weltanschauung of Nietzsche, especially in the late books, and that Nietzsche at any rate believed that his own habit of forming personal rather than intellectual attachments to those whom he considered great, such as Wagner, Schopenhauer, Zarathustra, was a Platonic or Socratic trait. We should also note how Nietzsche really puts forward a number of Platonic or Socratic suggestions, as for example the Academy, as his own, and how he, like Socrates, is convinced that men only need to know in order to be better and happier than they are now.

Some of this we have seen already: but there is one aspect of the Socratic problem which I deliberately did not discuss before, since it is far more relevant in this present position. This reiteration of Nietzsche's resemblance to Socrates leads up to the most remarkable of all Nietzsche's hesitations and self-doubts, which would indeed lose all its significance unless it is quite clear that the two men are intimately connected.

This doubt is involved in Nietzsche's Socratic ideal of the great teacher. We have seen already that Nietzsche resembled Socrates very closely in this point, that he was full of the pride of a teacher in his responsibility, and loved that pride and responsibility. We have also mentioned that he is full of fear that, like any other teacher of difficult things, he may not be understood, that "in certain circumstances he can be as great a curse to men as he ought to have been a blessing". For it is not what he is, but what other men think of him that will matter, that will influence the world: and therefore he must take care that their opinion of him is not merely correct, but *as profitable to them as it can be*.

The influential man, being really just an image in the minds of others, is bound to concern himself, even to torment himself, as to whether he is displaying the proper image for other men to see, and to profit by;—and whether he ought to.

Deeply rooted in Nietzsche is the principle of *not saying too much*: not merely on the mystic grounds connected with the religion of Dionysus; but for this more definite and logical reason that one can easily say more than it is good for ordinary people to hear. He says in another letter:

It is the form which my humanity takes, *to live in beautiful silence about my final purposes*; *and moreover* it is also the part of wisdom and self-preservation. What duties grow out of my way of thought ...this one I should break, and that one ruin...it is very possible that one day I shall become dumb, out of love for mankind!

Here we reach the heart of our problem: "To live in beautiful silence about my final purposes". It sounds curious, even suspicious, as if Nietzsche's public teaching did not display his real sentiments. But this "lie as love of humanity on the part of the man who knows", as the *Zarathustra* fragments call it, is part of the attitude of Socrates (so Nietzsche says), and this will double our suspicion, if we are already convinced that Socrates and Nietzsche are always close, and often identified.

Two of Nietzsche's aphorisms about Socrates bear upon this. The first is from *Die fröhliche Wissenschaft*.

The dying Socrates. I admire the bravery and wisdom of Socrates in everything which he did, said—and did not say. This mocking and erotic monster and ratcatcher of Athens, who made the most high-spirited young men tremble and sob, was just as great in keeping silence. I would that he had also been silent in the last moment of his life—perhaps then he would belong to an even higher order of spirits. Whether now it were death or the poison or piety or malice—something or other loosened his tongue in that moment, and he said: "O Crito, I owe Asclepius a cock". This ridiculous and fearful "last word" means for him, who has ears to hear: "O Crito, life is a sickness". Is it possible? A man like him, who had lived serenely and like a soldier before the eyes of all—was a pessimist! He had only just faced life with a brave countenance, and all the days of his life had concealed his final judgment, his innermost feeling. Socrates, Socrates suffered from life!...

This may be a very far-fetched argument of Nietzsche, but its peculiarity and significance cannot be exaggerated. However, in *Zur Genealogie der Moral* there is the other section, "Das Problem des Sokrates", which is no less remarkable. It is very much longer, so that I do not propose to quote it in full, but to give the gist of it, reinforced by a certain amount of quotation.

All the wisest people, Nietzsche begins, no matter to what epoch they belonged, have had the same opinion about life: "It is no good". Even Socrates, when he died, revealed that he considered life to be just a sickness, in the words: "Life—that means a long sickness: I owe the Saviour Asclepius a cock". But is it really life that is wrong? Is it not more probable that the wise men, the philosophers, are themselves sick, decadent? Yes, says Nietzsche, that is so, and I found it out by studying Socrates and Plato, who are the great decadents of Greece. The value of life cannot in fact be estimated at all, and if a man says that life is bad, he simply reveals that he is bad.

Socrates was a man from the lowest dregs of society. "Sokrates war Pöbel." Not only that, but he was the ugliest man in Greece; and to be ugly, among Greeks, is almost a proof that a man is not a Greek. Was Socrates a Greek at all?

Was he the physiological type of a decadent or a criminal? At any rate we have the story of the foreigner who recognised him as a criminal, and told him so; to whom Socrates merely replied: "You know me, sir". He suffered from aural hallucinations, and called them his "Daimonion", as we all know. That is one more sign of decadence.

The consequence of Socrates' activity was that Greek taste was revolutionised. It turned to Dialectics, lost all its former aristocratic qualities, and adopted those habits which had formerly been accounted plebeian. "Socrates was the clown who made himself be taken seriously: what really happened there?" He chose to make himself powerful by Dialectics because he had no other means to do so. It is a poor instrument, but the only one available for such as Socrates. Is his use of this one weapon an expression of class-consciousness, "Pöbel-Ressentiment", Revenge?

But Socrates did not merely repel, in spite of his repellent qualities: he attracted too. How? By inventing a new kind of field for the love of rivalry which was at the heart of the Greek character. "He fascinated, by stirring the agonal instinct of the Greeks—he brought a variant into the wrestling contests between young men and youths."

He did more. He saw very deep into the hearts of those around him; and discovered that they *needed* him, for they were all as decadent as he. "Everywhere the instincts were in anarchy: everywhere people were five steps removed from excess: the *monstrum in animo* was the general danger. The instincts desire to make the tyrant; one must invent a counter-tyrant, who is stronger." Now Socrates himself had discovered this counter-tyrant. When the foreigner told him of the evil passions revealed by his face, he admitted that it was so: but he added something more: "I became the master over them all". Therein lay half his fascination for an age like his. He had discovered the counter-tyrant, *reason*.

He did not see the danger he was running. He did not really succeed in making reason the tyrant—he could not succeed. Instead of becoming "reasonable", "vernünftig", he and his contemporaries became "absurd-vernünftig";

because they confined their application of the term Reason to certain things which were in fact not reasonable.

Nietzsche concludes thus. Socrates fascinated by appearing to be a physician, a saviour. *He failed, because it is not possible to step outside one's own circle, decadent or not, in order to prescribe for its ills.* That which he assumed to be a remedy was only another manifestation of the disease.

Socrates was a misunderstanding; the whole ethics of improvement, even the Christian, was a misunderstanding...the harshest daylight, reasonableness at any price, life bright, cold, cautious, conscious, without instinct, in resistance to instinct, was all itself only a sickness, another sickness—and by no means a return to "Virtue", to "Health", to "Happiness"...to *have to* fight against the instincts, that is the formula for decadence: as long as life is ascending, happiness is at the same time instinct.

And Socrates, as we have seen before, saw that. He *wished* to die; he made the Athenians kill him. "Socrates is no doctor, he said quietly to himself: here death alone is doctor...Socrates himself was only sick for a long time."

It cannot be proved that these two remarkable sections refer to Nietzsche himself as much as to Socrates, or instead of Socrates: but we remember how Nietzsche claims that he habitually spoke so of others when he meant himself, and how we have shown that he is extremely close to Socrates, and to Socrates' so-called decadence. And beside these two we can set another passage (from *Der Wille zur Macht*) in which Nietzsche mentions neither Socrates nor himself, but only the Ideal Philosopher. But have we not concluded that the Ideal Philosopher is something between Nietzsche himself, and Socrates, and Zarathustra? Let us see what he says. It is certainly curious enough.

Assuming that one thinks of a philosopher as a great teacher, mighty enough to draw up to himself from his lonely height long chains of generations from below, then one must also allow him the awful privileges of the great teacher. A teacher never says what he thinks himself, but only that which he thinks about a thing in relation to the advantage of him whom he is teaching. In this masquerade he must not be discovered; it is part of his eminence that people shall believe in his honesty....Such a teacher is beyond good and evil; but no one must know it.

But Socrates is Nietzsche, at least he often is. And here? Are we to suppose that Nietzsche, too, diagnosed life as "a sickness", but *did not say it*? I cannot but suppose that the last quotation, from *Der Wille zur Macht*, refers both to Nietzsche and Socrates, the great Teachers, and perhaps to the pre-Socratics as well. Only Zarathustra or Nietzsche is strong enough "from his lonely height to draw up long chains of generations from below". But why should the teacher, why should Zarathustra, never say what he really thinks, but only what he thinks in relation to the advantage of those whom he instructs? Is it because life is really not only terrible, as the Dionysiac knows, but hopeless? Because Nietzsche, like Socrates, does not believe, but pretends? Because he is an insincere prophet, at heart a pessimist, complete and perfect, a decadent, a disbeliever in life?

Probably not: although it is impossible to prove the matter either way. I do not think we have a right, on the evidence, to convict Nietzsche of continual and habitual and deliberate insincerity in his professed Weltanschauung: but I do think we have plenty of evidence to prove that he was often attacked by disbelief, and often troubled by "Sehnsucht" and doubt. When he says things like this, he means them for the moment, but perhaps—probably—not for always. For he is in all things an inconsistent and temperamental character, swayed in all sorts of queer directions, from time to time, by the circumstances of the moment; and we cannot tie him down to a statement as we could a more level-headed and systematic thinker. But if we cannot prove him out of his own mouth to have been a despairer *malgré soi*, we have perhaps shown that his view of life is not that of an optimist in the proper sense of the term, and that his advice and his Weltanschauung offer a poor prospect for most of us, and probably for all of us.

CHAPTER VIII

Conclusion

IN the introduction to this book I wrote that I would try, in a short final chapter, to summarise the conclusions reached: but now that I come to do so I feel far more impressed by the many points of interest which it has not been possible to raise, and by the unexplored possibilities for fruitful discussion which have presented themselves during the years which my work has taken. If then, in the following, and final, pages, I launch forth, after a very brief summary, into an examination of a few fresh details, I trust that it may be forgiven me: for the dominant feeling with which any student of Nietzsche must take leave of him is that, whatever may have been said or suggested, the half, and that no doubt the more important half, has not been told.

If however I am first to summarise, then I think that the main conclusion would be this: that the influence of the Classics, and especially of the early Greek philosophers, upon Nietzsche, has never been overrated, just as his influence upon the development of several branches of scientific study[1] has seldom or never been put too high: that on the other hand the influence upon him of other factors, and notably of the tradition or traditions of German civilisation, has constantly, though quite intelligibly, been overrated.[2] Intelligibly, because in the first place a quite natural patriotic pride, or something like it, continually tends to vitiate, or at least over-influence, the judgments of generally admirable German

---

[1] The first such branch which occurs to one is of course Classical Philology, where Nietzsche's influence has certainly been very great: but it is equally true that he has profoundly affected the whole tendency of modern literary criticism, and that the modern science, now so prominent in Germany, of "Geistesgeschichte", while it owes much to Dilthey and others, is to some extent a product of Nietzsche's ideas and criticisms.

[2] Most conspicuously by Bertram.

scholars, and in the second place, because Nietzsche did in
fact exercise a profound influence upon Germany for some
twenty or thirty years, so that there is a natural though illogical tendency for a German critic to conclude that he is
essentially German, an argument from effect to cause which
is quite pardonable.

But if plausible reasons can be urged both for the mental
attitude which impels a critic to claim Nietzsche as genuinely,
deeply German, and for the actual arguments which such a
critic will put forward, we are nevertheless not bound, and
not likely, to be impressed either by the one or by the other.
For the essential points in Nietzsche's final Weltanschauung,
though undoubtedly evolved to some extent under the inevitable pressure of his environment, and though also undoubtedly affected in great part by strains of influence which
do not proceed from Greece, are derived to an astonishingly
high degree from Greek thought, and especially, as we have
seen, from pre-Socratic philosophy. We have seen that
Nietzsche is not always willing to acknowledge such a debt,
as for instance in the matter of Recurrence, that he desires to
appear, not as "German", but as original: but if he does not
mainly derive his "philosophy of Dionysus", his theory of
the cycles in which the universe moves, his ethical position,
and even the conception of the Superman, from ideas which
he must have met in his classical studies, then the coincidences involved in certain parallelisms are quite intolerable.

But whereas the chief single influence upon Nietzsche was
that of the pre-Socratics, there are a number of points in
which, as we have seen, he is nearly related to Socrates and
Plato: although he is a fervent and almost unremitting critic
of their work and its effects, yet his beliefs concerning the
rôle of the philosopher in civilisation, and his ambitions to
fill that rôle, are such as one would only expect to find in
their pupil.

Of other points in which Nietzsche is connected with Greek
civilisation some have been discussed in the course of this
study, some have been left out altogether. The most interesting of these latter is the relationship—surprisingly close

and real—in which Nietzsche stands to the Epicureans : this I hope soon to discuss in another place. Apart from such matters, innumerable references to details in Greek literature or history are to be found on almost every page in Nietzsche's work from first to last : it would be quite impossible to include them in any book without causing it to run to an altogether inordinate length, and destroying all pretence at unity.

We have seen that our debt to Nietzsche at the present day is not slight, but we have also seen that it is not that which he himself intended. He is not, as he supposed himself, and as his (now few) undiscriminating admirers believe, a great constructive thinker. I have detailed reasons for supposing that any attempt to put his teaching into practice as he seems to desire would almost certainly lead to chaos ; that in a world swayed by his unrestricted will to power there would be little chance of even a physical development of men, none of a mental ; that incessant wars and upheavals, such as charac-terised the sixth century in Greece, will not bring about a progression of mankind, but a retrogression. Even in Greece it is far more likely that the advance of civilisation was due to the trading, colonising, and exploring adventurers than to the ceaseless small wars which were ruinous to the land, and hateful to all who suffered from them. It is true that as a rule Nietzsche does not literally advocate indiscriminate warfare ; but I cannot see that very different results would arise from applying in practice the principle that strife, in and for itself, is good. Moreover, Nietzsche's will to power leads nowhere ; and in this fact by itself lies (or seems to lie) a condemnation of his thought, for he has to demand, with great urgency and an effort at logical proof, an infinite succession of cosmoi, in which there is no variation whatever, for he can find no other aim or end of existence. With the ideal of a biological and mental advance of man there is no reason to quarrel, for man, as he is, is still generally a poor creature, in body and mind alike.

If the first key to understanding Nietzsche is to realise that he depends upon the pre-Socratics, and upon Socrates and Plato, more than upon anything else, then the second thing which must always be borne in mind is that he underwent a violent reaction against the period in which he lived, a period which others besides him have found intolerable. The society, politics, and religion which he attacks are not those of to-day, but those of the 'seventies and 'eighties, a period distinguished, no doubt, for many virtues, but not for broadmindedness, toleration, or depth of thought. We must remember too that in Germany the victory over France, and the resulting imperial greatness, for which the nation was probably unfitted, certainly unprepared, had evoked an extravagant self-esteem, which, however contemptible, is not beyond the comprehension of an unprejudiced observer, since it was in great part merely a temporary outburst of long-suppressed national pride. David Strauss was not a manifestation of culture, and those who accepted the ideas for which he stood were no doubt condemned as not understanding the rudiments of civilisation: but it does not follow that Nietzsche, in attacking him and his, was in all respects accurate or just, any more than he was, when criticising Christianity, in selecting Simeon Stylites as its typical representative.

Yet Nietzsche really deserved well of his contemporaries. They were dangerously self-satisfied, on rather slight grounds, and they needed to be disturbed. Nietzsche questioned nearly everything that they believed or did. His questioning was searching, and generally valuable: yet he did not answer many of his own questions, though he believed that he had answered them all. He dispensed with logical argument, relying upon instinct and eloquence to define and explain where explanation was needed, but these weapons did not always serve him well. Nevertheless he is at his worst when he attempts to prove his contentions scientifically; and as hierophant or epigrammatist he could often shed light upon problems which had caused great difficulty to careful and deserving thinkers. This we see in regard to the origins of Greek tragedy, where Nietzsche, by pure instinct, hit upon something very valuable, in defiance of all the established authorities and methods.

There he was at his best: but the conception of a universe which moves in identical cycles is, as we have seen, much less defensible. That life is will to power, and nothing else, is a more reasonable proposition, though Nietzsche's applications are again rather superficial and epigrammatic. It is certainly impossible to dismiss all the manifestations of impulses like religion as mere desire to increase power, however true it may be that this desire is sometimes—perhaps often—present in them. Christianity, which has brought power and honour and spiritual authority to some of its priests, has brought hardship and contempt to others; and the motives which Nietzsche attributes to every priest of every religion have been utterly absent from very many of them. It may conceivably be true that the Christian churches have done much evil, and little good, but Nietzsche does not prove it, while the benefits which they have undoubtedly conferred on civilisation are entirely ignored, or perversely condemned.

It is difficult, also, to sympathise with Nietzsche's admiration for heedless selfish strength, for it is apparently almost an instinct in us to feel that the poor and unfortunate have some claim on our attention. It is true that the kind of sympathy which he attacks so furiously is an almost intolerable perversion, but in point of fact it is not sympathy at all. The man who secretly rejoices in the misfortunes of others, who "makes himself a good afternoon out of his neighbours' sorrows" is not what is meant by a sympathetic man, nor is he the object of admiration, but Nietzsche, when discussing the nature, and the dangers, of sympathy, never seems to understand anything else by the word.

Nietzsche's attitude to women has evoked much criticism, some of which he deserves, though there is no need to accuse him of secret immorality, as some of his less scrupulous German enemies have done. In decisively separating men and women, and in assigning to women a lower and more limited sphere in the world, Nietzsche was going against a strong current in modern thought. He has brought much retribution upon his head, although many of his most fervent admirers are (or were) women. But if one accepts his hypothesis, then his attitude to women is less illogical than one might expect. Their place in the world is to him quite definite and clear. They are there to produce better and better children—not more and more children—and to comfort, cheer, assist and satisfy the men, who have to bear the greater part of the fight to increase power and to improve the race. Feminine education, female equality, and so on, are naturally anathema to him. Women are an ornament to life, not one of its serious ingredients. At the present time people do not on the whole believe this, and they are probably right. Yet it is difficult to maintain that the place of men and women in the world can ever be quite the same: and it is likely that the more extreme feminists are deluded. But is there really anything to cause offence in the statement that the highest woman is a higher being than the highest man, though rarer?

In the course of this investigation there has arisen another problem, which I have discussed in Chapter VII. This is the question of Nietzsche's sincerity. I have mentioned certain reasons which have led me, against the opinions of many other critics, but following Bertram, to doubt whether he really was sincere; and the more I reflect on the point, the more serious my doubts become. The point which led me to ask the question occurred in connection with Socrates, but there is another signpost in the same direction. It has been remarked that though Nietzsche was often unfair, he was never so unfair as when dealing with Christianity. It would probably be possible to show how the tendency to condemn Christianity more and more violently grew upon him steadily throughout his life. Is it possible that here too Nietzsche was saying that which he did not believe? Did he really find it impossible to rid himself of the last traces of that which he wished to believe to be superstitious, crippling and bad? Was he only able to urge others to reject a religion which he attacked with all the more exaggeration, since he himself did not believe what he said? He said that he was an incarnation of his father. Could he never exorcise his father's religious influence? Can one believe that that influence even gained power during the last frantic years of his lonely disappointed life? Was his final breakdown a consequence of his inability to shake off a religion which he hated and feared, but could not in his heart deny? If one concludes that Nietzsche did not really believe in his philosophy of life, one can believe this too: and I think that the almost inexplicable ferocity of *Der Antichrist* and *Ecce homo*, like the queer vein of superstition which occurs every now and again, is more explicable on this assumption than on any other. If Nietzsche was superstitious in some things, he may well have been superstitious in religion, though fighting desperately against it: in which case the madness of his last works was the madness of despair.

Finally a few words concerning Nietzsche's connection with German civilisation and his place in the German intellectual and literary tradition; on which subject infinitely more could be said than I have been able to say within the limits of this necessarily short book, where I have primarily been concerned with other aspects of his work. A thorough and unbiassed examination of the connection, undertaken by a non-German critic, would be a most valuable contribution to the study of Nietzsche. But it would have to begin by asking some very difficult and very disputable questions. What is German civilisation? Is there really something which we may call "der deutsche Geist", and, if there is, what are its essential characteristics? Nietzsche certainly believed that "der deutsche Geist" was something perceptible and definable, and at one period in his life he held that it contained, or had contained, elements of value. "I am afraid", he said, in the first *Unzeitgemässe Betrachtung*, "of the suppression, yes, the extirpation of the German spirit to the advantage of the German empire". So then, even if he usually appears as a harsh, uncompromising, unfair critic of his countrymen's attitude to life, and of their recent traditions, he does at least consider that at some time in the past (in fact, up to the time of Goethe, "the last German, for whom I have any respect") there existed a German civilisation which deserved respect and perpetuation.

And as a matter of fact it is not hard to see who were his intellectual predecessors in Germany. Goethe and Schiller,

Hölderlin and Stifter,[1] these and a few other names from the past, together with some contemporaries like Rohde and Burckhardt, represent Nietzsche's taste in Germanic civilisation, and it is undoubtedly by these above all that he was influenced, in so far as the Germanic past and present influenced him at all. That in his admiration for "natural" man, primitive man, the "blond beast", there is something derived from suggestions, however superficial, out of that past, or from memories of the heroic sagas, it would be impossible to deny, even when we see what a different result (different, that is, in all but its most superficial aspects) has been produced upon very different minds in the Germany of 1933 by the same suggestions and memories. It is of course impossible to believe that the new "national Germany" which we now see arising can keep a place for Nietzsche in its Pantheon, except by grossly misinterpreting him: for essentially he is no more German or Germanic than Wieland.[2] The resemblances between him and the modern German patriots are superficial, and no greater contrast is possible than appears between the turgid rhetorical sentimentality (Romanticism applied in practice), which is once more swaying a movement in German life (as it did, for example, in the Sturm und Drang), and on the other hand the enthusiastic, vigorous, noisy, but essentially unsentimental, and (within certain largely self-imposed limitations) clear-sighted intellectual force of Nietzsche, who had learned more from the South than from the North. For Germans are rarely good critics or good stylists; and, as we have noted more than once, it is as a critic and a stylist, and only as these, that Nietzsche excels.

[1] *Der Nachsommer* was one of Nietzsche's favourite books.
[2] Or than Schiller: but the legend that Schiller is the great German national poet—long exploded by unbiassed scholars like J. G. Robertson—will no doubt be given a fresh lease of life.

Select Bibliography

I. NIETZSCHE'S WORKS AND LETTERS.

(a) Editions of his works.

Musarion Monumental-Ausgabe. 22 volumes. Munich, 1920–.
Critical edition in 5 volumes by the Nietzsche-Archive. Leipzig,
1924.
Klassiker-Ausgabe. 9 volumes, edited by the Nietzsche-Archive.
Leipzig, 1922.
Taschenausgabe, with Introduction by Frau E. Förster-Nietzsche.
Leipzig, 1917.
English translation, edited by Dr O. Levy. Edinburgh and London,
1900–1913.

(b) Letters.

To his mother and sister. 2 vols., edited by Frau E.Förster-Nietzsche.
Leipzig, 1909.
To Peter Gast, edited by Peter Gast. Leipzig, 1924.
To Erwin Rohde, edited by Frau Förster-Nietzsche and Fritz Schöll.
Leipzig, 1923.
To Franz Overbeck, edited by Dr R. Oehler and C. A. Bernouilli.
Leipzig, 1916.
The Nietzsche-Wagner correspondence, edited by Frau Förster-
Nietzsche. (An English translation of this by Caroline V. Kerr.
London, 1922.)

II. WORKS OF CRITICISM AND INTERPRETATION.

Charles Andler: *Nietzsche, sa vie et sa pensée*. 6 vols. 1920–1931.
I. Beithan: *Nietzsche als Umwerter der deutschen Literatur*. (Dis-
sertation.) 1933.
H. Bélart: *Nietzsche et Richard Wagner*. 1907.
Ernst Bertram: *Nietzsche, Versuch einer Mythologie*. 1920.
G. Bianquis: *Nietzsche en France*. 1929.
G. Brandes: *Friedrich Nietzsche*. 1914.
M. Castiglioni: *Il poema eroico di Federico Nietzsche*. 1924.
E. Förster-Nietzsche: *Das Leben Nietzsches*. 1895, etc.
E. Förster-Nietzsche: *Der einsame Nietzsche*. 1914. (English trans-
lation, 1915.)
E. Förster-Nietzsche: *Der junge Nietzsche*. 1912. (English trans-
lation, 1912.)

E. Förster-Nietzsche: *Das Nietzsche-Archiv, seine Freunde und Feinde.* 1907.

Daniel Halévy: *La vie de Friedrich Nietzsche.* 1909.

Ernst Howald: *Nietzsche und die klassische Philologie.* 1920.

Carl Joel: *Nietzsche und die Romantik.* 1905.

B. Lachmann: *Protagoras, Stirner, Nietzsche.* (Bibliothek der Philosophie.) 1914.

H. Landsberg: *Nietzsche und die Literatur.* 1902.

H. Lichtenberger: *La philosophie de Nietzsche.* 1898. (Translated into German, 1899.)

R. M. Meyer: *Nietzsche, sein Leben und seine Werke.* 1913.

P. J. Möbius: *Über das Pathologische bei Nietzsche.* 1902.

F. Muckle: *Nietzsche und der Zusammenbruch der Kultur.* 1920.

M. A. Muegge: *Friedrich Nietzsche.* (In English.) 1912.

E. F. Podach: *Gestalten um Nietzsche.* 1932.

E. F. Podach: *Nietzsches Zusammenbruch.* 1930. (Also in English translation.)

Raoul Richter: *Friedrich Nietzsche, sein Leben und seine Werke.* 1903.

A. Riehl: *Friedrich Nietzsche, der Künstler und der Denker.* 1897.

L. I. Shestov: *Dostojewski und Nietzsche.* (Translated into German from Russian. 1924.)

L. I. Shestov: *Tolstoi und Nietzsche.* (Translated into German from Russian. 1923.)

G. Simmel: *Schopenhauer und Nietzsche, ein Vortragszyklus.* 1907.

Carl Spitteler: *Meine Beziehungen zu Nietzsche.* 1908.

H. Vaihinger: *Nietzsche als Philosoph.* Berlin, 1902.

Stefan Zweig: *Der Kampf mit dem Dämon* (*Hölderlin, Kleist, Nietzsche*). Volume II of series "Die Baumeister der Welt." 1920.

[N.B. There are in the British Museum Catalogue the titles of 122 different works of criticism concerning Nietzsche. Among these are included practically none of the many dissertations which have been published in Germany and elsewhere.]

Index of Proper Names

CAMBRIDGE: PRINTED BY WALTER LEWIS, M.A., AT THE UNIVERSITY PRESS